S.P.A. In-Depth
Speaking Proficiency Assessment

기출문제의 재구성
3년간 출제 된 SPA 기출문제 분석

- 현대기아자동차 그룹, LS신전 입사 승진 말하기 시험

- 문제집 한 권으로 SPA Master 하기!

- SPA 유형별 문제해결 Tip

- MP3 무료 다운로드　cafe.naver.com/hkspa

- 저자 직강의 해설 강의 Feed back 가능

SPA In-depth
기출문제의 재구성

지은이 David Cho
초판 1쇄 발행 2015년 5월 18일
펴낸곳 도서출판 미리내
등록번호 제 10-55호
등록년월일 1977년 9월 22일
발행인 김진식
주소 서울시 구로구 시흥대로 161길 26 B1
전화 070-8242-5411
홈페이지 www.mirinaeco.com
이메일 contact@mirinaeco.com
디자인 김윤이 ahzoa@naver.com
ISBN 978-89-7082-157-3
정가 20,000 원

....

Copyright ⓒ 2015 도서출판 미리내
이 책에 실린 모든 내용, 이미지, 디자인, 편집 구성은 출판사와 저자에게 저작권이 있습니다. 허락없이 내용의 일부나 전부를 복제할 수 없습니다.

서 문 PREFACE

미리내 SPA 교재의 목적은 한마디로 "SPA 시험 준비를 통한 올바른 영어 학습" 을 목표로 만들었습니다.

시중에 나온 교재 중에 제대로 SPA 학습법을 설명하고 있는 책이 없는 상황에서 SPA를 가장 잘 이해하고 있는 강사로서 많은 분들에게 도움을 주고자 집필하게 되었습니다.

SPA는 말하기 시험 Test 로서 책으로만 학습하기에는 한계가 있기 때문에 미리내 웹사이트 (www.mirinaeco.com)에 따로 듣기 자료를 업데이트하여 Interaction이 이루어지도록 만들었습니다.

또한 혼자 공부하는 한계를 넘어 전문강사의 피드백을 받을 수 있도록 언제든지 코칭 수업을 받을 수 있도록 만들었습니다.

미리내의 열정과 정신이 담긴 영어 학습은 단순한 공부를 넘어서 자신의 발전, 사회의 발전을 꿈꾸고 더욱더 살기 좋은 사회를 이룩하도록 항상 노력합니다.

2015년 미리내 편집부

SPA 시험이란?

한국SPA위원회에서 주관하는 SPA (Speaking Proficiency Assessment) Test는 실제 비즈니스 현장에서의 영어사용능력을 평가하기 위해 개발된 실무 중심 형 영어구술능력평가 시험입니다.

SPA Test는 종합적인 평가요소 별 출제기준에 의해 문제은행 방식으로 출제
10분간 2명의 원어민 평가위원과 응시자가 서로 대답을 주고 받는 면대면 인터뷰 방식의 시험
질문이 이해 되지 않을 경우 질문을 하여 정확한 이해를 구할 수 있습니다.

시험 진행 방식

1. 시험 대기 시 연습 용 샘플자료 제공
   시험 대기 시 감독관이 Tablet PC로 샘플 문제를 듣고 연습할 수 있도록 샘플자료 제공

2. Warm Up 대화시간
   시험 시작 전 평가위원과 익숙해지기 위한 Warm Up 대화 시간이 1분 제공 (평가에 반영되지 않음)

3. SPA시험진행 (10분)

5 Speaking Tasks

Part 1	Part 2	Part 3	Part 4	Part 5
발음 (Pronunciation)	청취력과 답변능력 (L/C & Response)	어휘사용능력 (Vocabulary)	문장구성능력 (Grammar & Structure)	언어 구사능력 (Overall Fluency)
Accent (intonation and stress) Pace (flow and rhythm of speech)	Listening passage summarization Accuracy / relevance of response	Accuracy of vocabulary in context Incorporation of applicable advanced terms and phrases	Correct usage of parts of speech Verb tense accuracy / consistency Syntax and diction Sentence structure variety / complexity Incorporation of transition signals / phrases	Communicative comprehension Logical flow and clarity of response Demonstration of freedom of expression Confidence and poise

SPA Test는 발음(Pronunciation), 청취력과 답변내용(Listening Comprehension & Response), 어휘사용능력 (Vocabulary), 문장구성능력(Grammar & Structure), 언어구사능력(Overall Fluency) 등 종합적인 영어 활용 능력을 영역별로 측정하여 점수화되어 시험 결과를 제공합니다.

책의 특징

1. 총 209개의 기출문제를 통째로 한 권의 책으로 분석과 함께 만날 수 있습니다

2. SPA 파트 별 핵심분석을 Tip 과 Strategy 부분에서 파악할 수 있습니다.

3. 수준에 맞는 Basic & Advanced Answers

4. 빈번히 출제되는 SPA시험의 Category, Topic, Vocab 별 분석

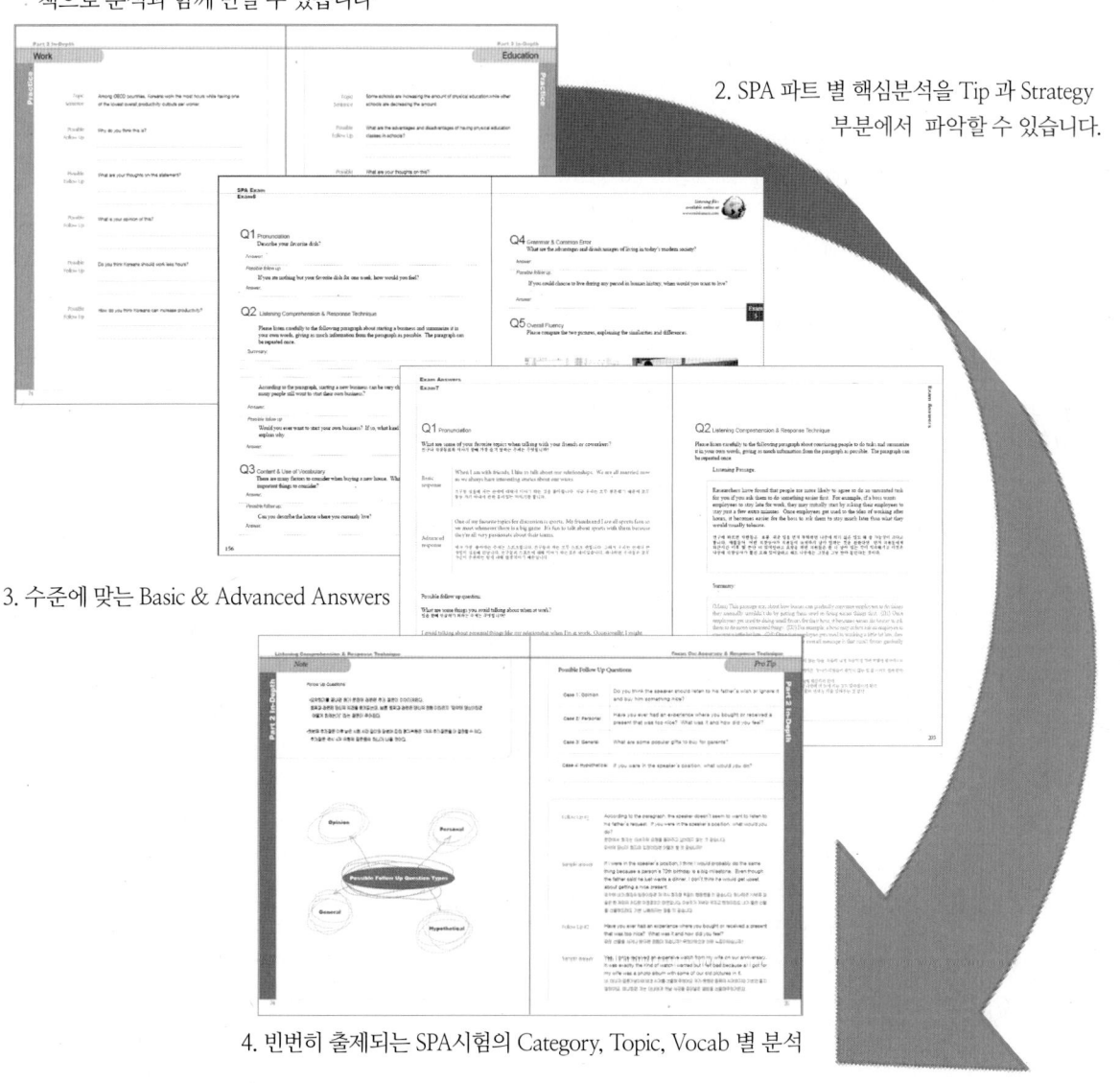

1권으로 끝내는
실전 SPA 시험 연습

SPA self evaluation & study method

미리내 웹사이트에서 Level별 Sample Answer를 들어보고 자신의 수준을 평가해보자

● Level 1 (SPA 0 ~15)
축하합니다. 적어도 당신은 Level 1의 대상자는 아닙니다. SPA에서는 Level 1의 점수는 사실상 전달해 주지 않습니다.

● Level 2 (SPA 16 ~ 24)
영어로 간단한 인사와 자기소개를 할 수 있으며 5W1H의 대답이 가능한 단계
Speaker is able to give one-word or short-phrase responses to the 5W1H questions.
Speaker may not fully comprehend all questions and thus respond to an unrelated Topic

이제 막 SPA 공부를 시작했거나 영어의 기초가 부족한 대상자입니다.
> Grammar와 Vocabulary 를 우선순위로 따로 공부하실 필요가 있습니다.
> SPA점수를 올리기 위해서는 무엇보다 본 책을 통해 SPA 유형에 익숙해지고 Part 3, 4 부분을 중점적으로 연습하면 단기간에 점수 향상도 가능합니다

● Level 3 (SPA 25 ~ 34)
간단한 생활영어가 가능하며, 발음과 문법에 초점을 맞추어 대화를 하는 단계.
Speaker is able to communicate basic ideas within limited contexts, but is unable to sufficiently support an opinion or statement. The majority of speaker's responses contain habitual grammatical, vocabulary and/or pronunciation errors.

어느 정도 영어 학습을 해 본 적이 있으나 원하는 점수대가 먼 고지로 느끼시는 대상자입니다.
이 레벨 역시 Grammar와 Vocabulary 를 우선순위로 공부하실 필요가 있습니다.
> Vocabulary 학습 시에는 단순하게 뜻을 외우는 것보다 문장에 적용해서 연습해보도록 합니다.
> Part 2에서 Main Point를 Catch하여 설명하는 것이 Key point인 레벨입니다.
> 원하는 SPA점수를 올리기 위해서는 본 책을 통해 SPA Part 2 문제에 답변을 해보고 자신이 부족한 부분을 분석해 보는 것을 권장합니다. 시간이 걸리더라도 자신의 답변의 문제점을 파악하여 연습하면 의외로 금방 원하는 점수에 도달 할 수 있습니다.

● Level 4 (SPA 35 ~ 49)
생활영어에 대한 전반적인 주제에 대해 대화가 가능하지만, 문법적 오류가 있는 단계.
Speaker is able to communicate basic ideas across a wide range of general conversational topics. Speaker is occasionally able to provide some elaboration, but responses still contain frequent grammatical, vocabulary and/or pronunciation errors.

기본적인 생활영어에는 자신 있게 대답할 수 있는 대상자입니다.
> 기출문제 유형에 익숙해지고 advanced response skill을 따라 해보는 것을 권장합니다.
> 회화에서의 접속사 연습, Idiom, 발음 등을 연습하여 원어민 같이 따라해보는 연습이 필요합니다

● **Level 5 (SPA 50 ~ 64)**
비즈니스 회화가 가능하나, 심도 있는 언어 표현은 부족한 단계.
Speaker is able to express general ideas successfully but with limited elaboration.
Speaker may lack the vocabulary and complex grammatical structures necessary to
deliver in-depth responses with accuracy.

영문과 졸업 혹은 해외 유학을 다녀와서 영어에 자신 있는 대상자입니다.
　평소에 생각해보지 못한 질문이 나오는 SPA 질문에 익숙해집니다.
　고급 단어의 숙지와 함께 언어 스킬을 연습하며 Detail 하게 대답하는 연습이 필요합니다.

이 교재를 통해 Part별 Scoring 위주로 대답하는 것을 연습합니다.

● **Level 6 (SPA 65 ~ 74)**
비즈니스의 다양한 상황에 따른 Formal 한 회화를 구사할 수 있는 단계
Speaker is highly intelligible and able to express ideas and elaborate on responses
effectively. Speaker may occasionally use imprecise vocabulary, grammar and/or
pronunciation, but these errors do not hinder general comprehensibility.

● **Level 7 (SPA 75 ~ 84)**
Native와는 구분이 되지만 회화에 대해 어려움이 전혀 없는 단계
Speaker's proficiency approaches the native level. Speaker delivers well-developed
responses and explanations. At the advanced level, thespeaker's use of imprecise
vocabulary, grammar and/or pronunciation is rare and negligible

● **Level 8 (SPA 85 ~ 96)**
Native Speaker 및 영어가 모국어인 교포 수준의 영어회화 단계.
Speaker's proficiency is equivalent to that of a native speaker. Speaker demonstrates
complete control of language and freedom of expression

Level 6 이상의 학습자는 오랜 기간 영어를 학습하고 있거나 해외 거주 경험이 있는 대상자입니다.
보통 교포이상 Native Speaker가 받을 수 있는 점수의 레벨입니다. 그러나 아무리 Native Speaker
일지라도 만점을 받기는 어렵습니다. 왜냐하면 SPA는 언어시험이 아닌 Communication Test 라는
것을 명심해야 합니다. 이 레벨의 학습자는 이 교재를 SPA 유형 이해로 참고하면 반드시 실수 없이
좋은 점수를 얻어 가실 수 있습니다

How to Study for the SPA?

```
본문에 나온 Tip, Overview,,          모르는 부분은
Strategy를 숙지                      www.mirinaeco.com 게시판을
                                    통해 질문하거나 feedback
                                    service 를 받는다.
         │                                   │
         ▼                                   ▼
Part 별 연습문제를                    자신이 대답한 녹음 음성을
모두 풀어보고 기출문제                들어보고 본 교재의 Sample
풀어보기                             Answer와 비교
         │                                   │
         ▼                                   ▼
모든 연습은 자신의                    기출문제는 실제 시험 보듯이
목소리를 직접 녹음해보고              시간을 재면서 대답
다시 들어본다
```

Feedback Service
SPA 전문강사와 원하는 시간에 Coaching을 받아 볼수 있도록 서비스를 제공합니다.

Online 모의 Test
Skype를 통해 10분간 Test 실시 후 20분간 피드백을 바로 받아 볼 수 있습니다.

* 모든 서비스는 www.mirinaeco.com에서 회원등록 후 가능합니다.

문의: contact@mirinaeco.com / 070-8242-5411

Table of Contents

Part 1 In-Depth..13

    01 Preview
    02 Overview
    03 Tip
    04 Q1 Sample
    05 Strategy
    06 Note
    07 Pro Tip

Part 1 Practice..20

    01 Describing Preferences
    02 Who / What Questions
    03 Recommendations
    04 Frequency Questions
    05 Future Plans

Part 2 In-Depth..43

    01 Preview
    02 Overview
    03 Tip
    04. Q2 Sample
    05. Strategy
    06 Note
    07 Pro Tip

Part 2 Practice..50

    01 Personal Narrative
    02 Pop Culture
    03 Famous People
    04 Work Environment
    05 Research / Study
    06 Technology
    07 Transportation
    08 Currant Affairs

Table of Contents

Part 3 In-Depth 83

- 01 Preview
- 02 Overview
- 03 Tip
- 04 Q3 Sample
- 05 Strategy
- 06 Note
- 07 Pro Tip

Part 3 Practice 88

- 01 Finance
- 02 Travel
- 03 Work
- 04 Education
- 05 Relationship
- 06 Technology
- 07 Trends
- 08 Health

Part 4 In-Depth 113

- 01 Preview
- 02 Overview
- 03 Tip
- 04. Q4 Sample
- 05. Strategy
- 06 Note
- 07 Pro Tip

Part 4 Practice 120

- 01 Hypothetical / Role-play Scenario
- 02 Making a Decision
- 03 Making a List
- 04 Best / Worst, Most / Least
- 05 Advantages / Disadvantages
- 06 Have you ever ?

Table of Contents

Part 5 In-Depth..139

    01 Preview
    02 Overview
    03 Tip
    04. Q5 Sample
    05. Strategy

Part 5 Practice..142

    01 Description
    02 Bar Graph
    03 Pie Graph
    04 Line Graph
    05 Role Play
    06 Preference

SPA Exams..157

    SPA Exam 1
    SPA Exam 2.
    SPA Exam 3
    SPA Exam 5
    SPA Exam 6
    SPA Exam 7
    SPA Exam 8

SPA Exams Answer Key..175

    SPA Exam 1 Answers
    SPA Exam 2 Answers
    SPA Exam 3 Answers
    SPA Exam 4 Answers
    SPA Exam 5 Answers
    SPA Exam 6 Answers
    SPA Exam 7 Answers
    SPA Exam 8 Answers

Must Know SPA Vocab list...226
Transition Phrases to Boost your Score..229

SPA In-Depth
Part 1

Pronunciation
Focus on: Accent / Pace

Question Categories:
- Describing Preferences
- Who / What Questions
- Recommendations
- Frequency Questions
- Future Plans

Part 1: Pronunciation

Preview

Q1 Do you prefer waking up early or late?

Follow up — Can you explain why?

Follow up — What is your normal morning routine like?

Overview

- Part 1의 배점은 12점이다.

- Accent (intonation and stress)와 Pace (flow and rhythm of speech)를 채점을 하게된다.

- 전체적으로 봤을때 큰 비중이 없는 파트이기 때문에 대부분 대답을 1분내외로 끝낼 수 있는 Simple Question을 물어보게 된다.

Tip

- 평소에 생각하지 않았던 아니면 기억나지 않는 경험, 선택, 설명 등을 물어볼 수가 있다. 꼭 진실을 말할 필요가 없으니 자신이 가장 자신있게 대답할 수 있는 답변을 정확하게 말하는 연습이 필요하다.

- 한국인들이 자주 하는 발음 실수 **f/p, l/r, z/j, b/v, s/sh, and s/th** 에 유의. 말을 하다가 잠시멈추거나 머뭇 거리지 않고 자연스럽게 이어 말한다.

Focus On: Pace / Accent

Sample

Q1

Do you prefer waking up early or late?

Response

I prefer waking up early.

Follow up Q #1

Can you explain why?

Response

I like to wake up early because it gives me more time to prepare for work.

Follow up Q #2

What is your normal morning routine like?

Response

First, I like to take a shower. Then, I brush my teeth. Next, I put on my outfit for the day. Afterwards, I eat some rice or cereal. Lastly, I say goodbye to my family and go to work.

Part 1: Pronunciation

Q1

Do you prefer waking up early or late?
아침에 일찍 일어나는 것과 늦게 일어나는 것 중 어느쪽을 선호하나요?

Response

I prefer waking up early.
아침에 일찍 일어나는 것을 선호합니다.

Strategy

- 왜 이러한 대답인 괜찮은 거죠? 너무 짧지 않나요?
  Part 1을 살펴보면 평소에 마주하게 되는 일상적인 질문이고 대답도 꽤 평범하다.

- 완벽한 대답을 하려고 너무 오래 생각하지 말것!

- 만약 짧은 답이 마음에 들지 않아 길게 말하고 싶으면 물론 대답에 세부사항을 더 집어 넣어 대답 수는 있다. (단 페이스를 유지하고 정확한 액센트로 말할 수 있어야 한다.)
  평가위원이 세부사항을 알고 싶다면 다음 페이지에 나오는 표와 같은 기준으로 세부사항을 물어볼 것이다.

- Follow up questions은 보통 5W1H 포맷 안에서 나오게 된다. 이러한 포맷 안에서 답을 연습해 나가는 것이 점수를 빠르게 올릴 수 있는 비법 이다.

Focus On: Pace / Accent

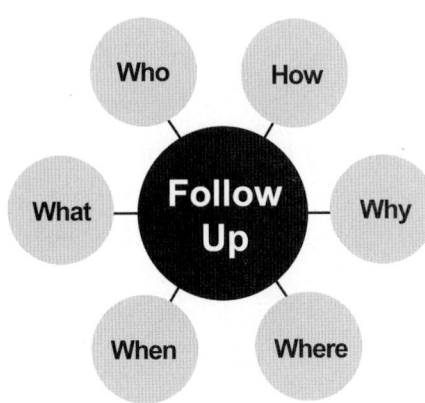

	Possible Question	Possible Response
Who	Who's the first person to wake up in your family?	My wife is normally the first person to wake up in my family. She likes to wake up early so that she can make breakfast for me.
What	What do you usually do after you wake up?	I usually go to the bathroom to take a shower and brush my teeth.
When	When do you usually wake up?	I usually wake up at around 6:30 in the morning.
Where	Where do you usually go after waking up?	I usually go straight to the bathroom to brush my teeth and take a shower.
Why	Why do you prefer waking up early?	I prefer waking up early because it gives me time to prepare for work.
How	How is waking up early better than waking up late?	Waking up early is better because I don't have to be in a rush for work.

Part 1: Pronunciation

Follow up #1　**Can you explain why?**
　　　　　　이유를 설명할 수 있습니까?

Response　　I like to wake up early because it gives me more time to prepare for work.
　　　　　　아침에 일찍 일어나는 것을 선호합니다. 왜냐하면 아침에 출근하기전에 준비할 시간을 충분히 가질 수 있으니까요.

- 'WHY'에 대한 질문은 평가위원이 다양한 방법으로 물어볼 수 있다.
  아래 다양한 방법들의 WHY 질문을 살펴보고 미리 대비해보도록 하자

Different ways to ask WHY

Can you explain why?

Can you explain why you prefer to wake up early?

Could you explain why?

Why do you prefer waking up early?

Why do you like waking up early?

What is/are the reason(s) why you prefer waking up early?

Response　　I like to wake up early because it gives me more time to prepare for work.

Focus On: Pace / Accent

Follow up #2	**What is your normal morning routine like?** 보통 아침의 일과가 어떻게 됩니까?
Response	First, I like to take a shower. Then, I brush my teeth. Next, I put on my outfit for the day. Afterwards, I eat some rice or cereal. Lastly, I say goodbye to my family and go to work. 먼저 샤워를 하고, 이를 닦은 후 외출복을 입습니다. 그런 다음 밥이나 씨리얼을 먹고 마지막으로 가족들에게 인사를 하고 출근합니다.

- 첫번째 대답의 디테일에 따라 평가위원은 추가적인 질문을 결정할 수 있다.
- SPA Part 1에서의 추가 질문은 대부분 처음 질문과 관련된 질문을 하게 된다.
- 평가위원은 당신의 개인적인 경험이나 의견을 묻기 때문에 이 부분에서 너무 세밀하게 생각할 필요는 없을 것이다.

Note

- 추가 질문에서 평가위원은 평가를 위한 적당한 대답을 들었으면 만족하고 바로 Part 2 문제로 지나가게 된다.

- 다음 페이지에 나오는 Possible Questions는 SPA에서 가장 자주 나오는 유형의 질문들이니 유형을 연습하고 대비하면 Part 1은 가뿐히 지나 갈 수 있을것이다.

- 질문들에 대해 먼저 자신의 답으로 연습을 해 본 후 어떤 추가 질문이 나올까 예상해본다.
  질문들에 대한 Sample 답안을 확인해보고 자신이 평가위원이라 생각해 본 후 5W1H 형식으로 추가질문을 만들어본다.

Part 1: Pronunciation

Describing Preferences

1. Do you prefer working in the morning or at night?

....

....

2. Do you prefer waking up early or late?

....

....

3. Do you prefer taking a shower in the morning or at night?

....

....

4. Do you prefer to sleep on a bed or on the floor?

....

....

5. Do you prefer driving a car to work or taking public transportation?

....

....

Focus On: Pace / Accent

Describing Preferences

Part 1 Practice

6. Do you prefer to speak on the phone or text message?

7. Do you prefer eating out or eating at home?

8. Do you prefer hot or cold weather?

9. Do you prefer coffee or tea?

10. Do you prefer summer or winter?

Describing Preferences

1. Do you prefer working in the morning or at night?

2. Do you prefer waking up early or late?

3. Do you prefer taking a shower in the morning or at night?

4. Do you prefer to sleep on a bed or on the floor?

5. Do you prefer driving a car to work or taking the public transportation?

6. Do you prefer to speak on the phone or text message?

7. Do you prefer eating out or eating at home?

8. Do you prefer hot or cold weather?

9. Do you prefer coffee or tea?

10. Do you prefer summer or winter?

1. 아침에 일하는 것과 밤에 일하는 것중 어느 것을 선호 합니까?

2. 일찍 일어나는 것과 늦게 일어나는 것중 어느 것을 선호 합니까?

3. 아침에 샤워하는 것과 저녁에 샤워하는 것중 어느 것을 선호 합니까?

4. 침대에서 자는 것과 바닥에서 자는 것중 어느 것을 선호 합니까?

5. 자가용을 타고 출근하는 것과 대중교통을 타고 출근하는 것중 어느 것을 선호 합니까?

6. 전화하는 것과 문자하는 것중 어느것을 선호 합니까?

7. 외식하는 것과 집에서 식사하는 것중 어느 것을 선호합니까?

8. 더운 날씨와 추운 날씨중에 어느 날씨를 선호합니까?

9. 커피나 차 중 어느 것을 선호합니까?

10. 여름이나 겨울 중에 어느 계절을 선호합니까?

Focus On: Pace / Accent

Describing Preferences

1. I prefer working in the morning because my mind is more clear after waking up.

2. I prefer waking up late because I usually sleep very late at night.

3. I prefer taking a shower in the morning because my hair is very messy when I wake up.

4. I prefer to sleep on the floor because it's better for keeping my back straight.

5. I prefer to take the public transportation because it can be very difficult to find parking.

6. I prefer to talk on the phone because it's easier to convey my feelings using my voice.

7. I prefer eating out because I don't have to worry about cleaning the dishes.

8. I prefer cold weather because I hate sweating.

9. I prefer tea more because it's healthier.

10. I prefer summer because the warm weather makes it easier to go out at night.

---

1. 아침에 일하는 것을 선호합니다. 왜냐하면 잠자고 나서 정신이 더 상쾌해지니까요.

2. 늦게 일어나는 것을 선호합니다. 왜냐하면 밤에 늦게 잠들기 때문입니다.

3.. 아침에 샤워하는 것을 선호합니다. 왜냐하면 아침에 일어나면 머리가 헝클어져있기 때문입니다.

4. 바닥에서 자는 것을 선호합니다. 왜냐하면 허리를 반듯하게 유지하는데 좋으니까요.

5. 대중교통을 이용하는 것을 선호합니다. 왜냐하면 주차장 찾기가 어렵기 때문입니다.

6. 전화사용하는 것을 선호합니다 목소리로 느낌을 전하기 쉽기 때문입니다.

7. 외식하는 것을 선호합니다. 왜냐하면 설거지 걱정이 없기 때문입니다.

8. 추운 날씨를 선호합니다. 왜냐하면 땀 흘리는 것을 싫어 하기 때문입니다.

9. 차 마시는 것을 선호합니다. 왜냐하면 더 건강하기 때문입니다.

10. 여름을 선호합니다. 왜냐하면 따뜻한 날씨라서 밤에 외출하기 좋기 때문입니다.

Part 1 Practice

Part 1: Pronunciation

Who / What Questions

1. What is your favorite snack?
   ....
   ....

2. What was your favorite type of music growing up?
   ....
   ....

3. What is the best restaurant in your city?
   ....
   ....

4. What do you enjoy the most about working?
   ....
   ....

5. What did you do for your last vacation?
   ....
   ....

Focus On: Pace / Accent

Who / What Questions

6. Who is your favorite musician?

   ....

   ....

7. Who helps you the most at work?

   ....

   ....

8. Who is the most important person in your life?

   ....

   ....

9. Who do you admire the most?

   ....

   ....

10. Who has been the biggest influence in your life?

    ....

    ....

Who / What Questions

1. What is your favorite snack?

2. What was your favorite type of music growing up?

3. What is the best restaurant in your city?

4. What do you enjoy the most about working?

5. What did you do for your last vacation?

6. Who is your favorite musician?

7. Who helps you the most at work?

8. Who is the most important person in your life?

9. Who do you admire the most?

10. Who has been the biggest influence in your life?.

1. 제일 좋아하는 과자는 무엇입니까?

2. 자라면서 가장 좋아했던 음악장르는 무엇입니까?

3. 당신의 도시에서 최고의 맛집은 어디입니까?

4. 일을하면서 어떤 것이 가장 즐겁습니까?

5. 지난 휴가때 무엇을 하였습니까?

6. 가장 좋아하는 뮤지션은 누구입니까?

7 직장에서 누가 가장 많이 도와줍니까?

8. 당신의 인생에서 가장 중요한 사람은 누구입니까?

9. 누구를 가장 존경합니까?

10. 누가 당신의 인행에 가장 큰 영향을 주었습니까?

Focus On: Pace / Accent
Who / What Questions

1. My favorite snack is Cheetos. It's been my favorite snack since I was little.

2. My favorite type of music was rock. I liked it because it matched my young energy level.

3. The best restaurant in my city is called Gyeongbokgong. It is a traditional Korean style restaurant located near Myeongdong.

4. What I enjoy the most about working is working with other people that have the same passion for my field of interest.

5. During my last vacation, I traveled to Jeju Island. We rented a boat and went fishing off the coast.

6. My favorite musician is Cho Yong Pil. He has a very nice voice.

7. My colleague Andrew helps me the most at work. We are on the same team so he always helps me with my projects.

8. My mother is the most important person in my life. She raised me and she still gives me good advice whenever I need it.

9. I admire my wife the most. Not only does she take care of me, she is also a great mother to my children.

10. My daughter has been the biggest influence in my life. As soon as she was born, I wanted to live my life for her.

---

1. 제일 좋아하는 과자는 치토스입니다. 어렸을때부터 가장 좋아하던 과자입니다.

2. 가장 좋아했던 음악은 락입니다. 어렸을적의 젊은 혈기와 맞아 떨어졌기 때문입니다.

3. 우리도시에서 최고의 맛집은 경복궁이라 불리는 명동 근처에 있는 한국전통 레스토랑입니다.

4. 일을하면서 가장 즐거운 것은 같은 관심 분야의 열정을 가진 사람들과 함께 일 하는 것입니다.

5. 지난 휴가때 제주도에 갔습니다. 배를 빌려서 해안가에서 낚시를 했습니다.

6. 가장 좋아하는 뮤지션은 조용필입니다. 그는 좋은 목소리를 가졌습니다.

7. 동료 앤드류가 저를 가장 많이 도와줍니다. 우리는 같은 팀이라서 그는 항상 제 프로젝트를 도와줍니다.

8. 어머니가 제 인생에 있어서 가장 중요합니다. 저를 길러주셨고 제가 필요할때마다 언제든지 조언을 해 주십니다.

9. 아내를 가장 존경합니다. 저를 챙겨 주는것 뿐 아니라 아이들에게 있어서도 훌륭한 이미니 입니다.

10. 제 딸이 제 삶에 있어서 가장 큰 영향을 끼쳤습니다. 딸을 낳자마자 저는 딸을 위해 살고 싶어졌습니다.

Recommendations

1. Can you recommend a healthy dinner meal?

   ....

   ....

2. Can you recommend a good place to visit in Korea?

   ....

   ....

3. Can you recommend the best way to succeed at work?

   ....

   ....

4. Could you recommend a good Korean dish for foreigners to try?

   ....

   ....

5. Could you recommend a good band to listen to?

   ....

   ....

Focus On: Pace / Accent

Recommendations

6. Could you recommend a movie that came out recently?

7. Would you recommend visiting your hometown to travelers?

8. Would you recommend buying a desktop computer or a laptop?

9. What would you recommend for a tourist traveling to Korea for the first time?

10. What sport would you recommend for exercise?

Recommendations

1. Can you recommend a healthy dinner meal?

2. Can you recommend a good place to visit in Korea?

3. Can you recommend the best way to succeed at work?

4. Could you recommend a good Korean dish for foreigners to try?

5. Could you recommend a good band to listen to?

6. Could you recommend a movie that came out recently?

7. Would you recommend visiting your hometown to travelers?

8. Would you recommend buying a desktop computer or a laptop computer?

9. What would you recommend for a tourist traveling to Korea for the first time?

10. What sport would you recommend for exercise?

1. 건강한 저녁식사를 추천해 주실 수 있습니까?

2. 한국에서 방문할 만한 좋은 장소를 추천해 주실 수 있습니까?

3. 직장에서 성공할 수 있는 최고의 방법을 추천해 주실 수 있습니까?

4. 외국인이 먹을 만한 한국 음식을 추천해 주실 수 있습니까?

5. 듣기 좋은 괜찮은 밴드를 추천해 주실 수 있습니까?

6. 최근에 개봉한 영화를 추천해 주실 수 있습니까?

7. 당신의 고향에 방문 할 만한 장소를 여행객들에게 추천해주실 수 있습니까?

8. 노트북과 데스크탑 컴퓨터중 어느 것을 추천 하십니까?

9. 한국을 처음 여행하는 여행객들에게 추천해 줄 것은 무엇입니까?

10. 운동하기에 어떤 스포츠를 추천해 주겠습니까?

Focus On: Pace / Accent

Recommendations

1. For a healthy dinner, I would recommend grilled salmon. It is very healthy and delicious.

2. Yes, I would recommend visiting Busan. The beaches there are very beautiful and the seafood is excellent.

3. The best way to succeed at work is to do exactly what your boss tells you to do.

4. Sure, I would recommend foreigners try bulgogi. It's a grilled beef dish that almost everyone enjoys eating.

5. I'd recommend listening to the Beatles. Most of their songs have a catchy melody that's easy to listen to.

6. I would highly recommend that you watch the Avengers II. The action scenes are spectacular!

7. No, I would not recommend my hometown to visitors. It's very boring there.

8. I would recommend buying a desktop because desktops are usually more powerful and cost a lot less.

9. I would recommend that they learn how to read hangeul. It's very easy to learn and it can be quite useful while traveling throughout Korea.

10. I would recommend swimming because it's a great workout for both your heart as well as your muscles.

---

1. 건강한 저녁을 위해서 그릴에 구운 연어를 추천합니다. 건강하며 맛있는 음식입니다.

2. 부산에 방문해볼 것을 추천합니다. 해변이 무척 아름답고 해산물 역시 매우 좋습니다.

3. 업무에서 성공을 거두는 최고의 방법은 직장상사가 당신에게 말한 것을 정확하게 해내는 것입니다.

4. 외국인에게 불고기를 추천합니다. 대부분의 사람들이 즐겁게 먹을 수 있는 구워먹는 소고기 요리 입니다.

5. 비틀즈를 추천합니다. 대부분의 노래들이 입안에 맴돌게 만들고 쉽게 들을 수 있는 음악입니다.

6. 어벤져스2 보는 것을 강력히 추천합니다. 액션 장면이 스펙타클 합니다!

7. 제 고향을 여행객 들에게 추천하지 않습니다. 매우 심심한 곳 이거든요.

8. 데스크탑 컴퓨터를 사는 것을 추천합니다. 왜냐하면 데스크탑이 보통 더 강력하고 값이 싸기 때문이죠.

9. 한글 읽는 방법을 배울 것을 추천합니다. 매우 배우기 쉽고 한국을 여행할때 꽤 편리합니다.

10. 수영하는 것을 추천합니다. 왜냐하면 심폐능력과 근육운동에 매우 좋으니깐요.

Part 1: Pronunciation

Frequency Questions

1. How often do you buy new clothes?
   ....
   ....

2. How often do you go out with friends?
   ....
   ....

3. How often do you change your hairstyle?
   ....
   ....

4. How often do you exercise?
   ....
   ....

5. How often do you travel outside your city?
   ....
   ....

Focus On: Pace / Accent

Frequency Questions

Part 1 Practice

6. How often do you eat out?

....

....

7. How often do you watch television?

....

....

8. How many times do you eat a day?

....

....

9. How many times have you changed your cellphone?

....

....

10. How frequently do you speak with your relatives?

....

....

Frequency Questions

1. How often do you buy new clothes?
2. How often do you go out with friends?
3. How often do you change your hairstyle?
4. How often do you exercise?
5. How often do you travel outside your city?
6. How often do you eat out?
7. How often do you watch television?
8. How many times do you eat a day?
9. How many times have you changed your cellphone?
10. How frequently do you speak with your relatives?

1. 얼마나 자주 옷을 삽니까?
2. 얼마나 자주 친구와 나가 어울립니까?
3. 얼마나 자주 헤어스타일을 바꿉니까?
4. 얼마나 자주 운동을 합니까?
5. 얼마나 자주 여행을 합니까?
6. 얼마나 자주 외식을 합니까?
7. 얼마나 자주 TV시청을 합니까?
8. 하루에 몇 끼를 드십니까?
9. 지금까지 몇 번 핸드폰을 바꾸었습니까?
10. 친척들과 얼마나 자주 이야기 합니까?

Focus On: Pace / Accent
Frequancy Questions

1. I usually buy new clothes twice a year. Once during winter and once during summer.

2. I go out maybe once or twice a week. We usually just meet at a restaurant to eat and drink together.

3. I hardly ever change my hairstyle. It has been the same since I was in college.

4. I exercise for about 30 minutes every morning. I usually just jog in my neighborhood.

5. I travel outside my city at least once a week. My girlfriend and I like to go to different parts of the country during the weekends.

6. I eat out once a day during lunch. When I'm not working, I like to eat at home.

7. I usually watch about an hour of television each day.

8. I usually only have two meals a day. I know I should eat more but I'm usually too busy.

9. I've changed my cellphone six times so far. I change it every two years.

10. I hardly ever speak with my relatives these days. They all live very far away so I've lost touch with most of them.

1. 보통 1년에 두 번 옷을 삽니다. 겨울에 한번 여름에 한 번 옷을 구입합니다.

2. 일주일에 한 두번 밖에 놀러 나갑니다. 보통 나가면 함께 밥을 먹거나 술을 마십니다.

3. 저는 헤어스타일을 거의 바꾸지 않습니다. 대학교때부터 계속 같은 스타일 입니다.

4. 매일 아침 30분씩 운동을 합니다. 보통 동네에서 조깅을 뜁니다.

5. 적어도 일주일에 한 번은 여행을 갑니다. 여자친구와 저는 주말에 다른 지역에 가는 것을 좋아합니다.

6. 하루에 한번은 점심시간에 외식을 합니다. 일을 하지 않을때는 집에서 먹는것을 좋아합니다.

7. 보통 하루에 약 한 시간 정도 텔레비젼을 시청합니다.

8. 보통 하루에 두끼만 먹습니다. 더 먹어야 한다는 것을 알지만 너무 바빠서 시간이 없어요.

9. 지금까지 핸드폰을 6번 바꾸었습니다. 2년에 한 번씩 핸드폰을 교체합니다.

10. 요즘에 친척들과 거의 이야기를 하지 않습니다. 친척 모두 매우 먼 곳에 살고 있어서 대부분의 친척들과 연락이 끊겼습니다.

Part 1: Pronunciation

Future Plans

1. What are your plans for your next vacation?

   ....

   ....

2. What are your plans for retirement?

   ....

   ....

3. What are your career goals?

   ....

   ....

4. What do you plan to do this weekend?

   ....

   ....

5. What do you plan to do next Christmas?

   ....

   ....

Focus On: Pace / Accent

Future Plans

6. What do you hope to accomplish by the end of the year?

....

....

7. What kind of person do you want to become?

....

....

8. What will you do on your last day of work?

....

....

9. What will you do for your next birthday?

....

....

10. Where do you see yourself in 5 years?

....

....

Part 1: Pronunciation

Future Plans

1. What are your plans for your next vacation?

2. What are your plans for retirement?

3. What are your career goals?

4. What do you plan to do this weekend?

5. What do you plan to do next Christmas?

6. What do you hope to accomplish by the end of the year?

7. What kind of person do you want to become?

8. What will you do on your last day of work?

9. What do you want to do for your next birthday?

10. Where do you see yourself in 5 years?

1. 다음 휴가 계획은 무엇입니까?

2. 은퇴계획은 어떻게 세웠습니까?

3. 당신의 커리어 목표는 무엇입니까?

4. 이번 주말에 무엇을 할 계획입니까?

5. 다음 크리스마스의 계획은 무엇입니까?

6. 올해 말 까지 달성하고 싶은 것은 무엇입니까?

7. 어떤 사람이 되고 싶습니까?

8. 직장 마지막날에 무엇을 할 것 같습니까?

9. 다음 생일에 무엇을 하고 싶습니까?

10. 5년후에는 어떤 모습일 것 같습니까?

Focus On: Pace / Accent

Future Plans

1. I plan to go to Guam for my next vacation. I hear the water there is really clear.

2. When I save enough money for retirement, I plan to buy a house in Jeju-do and fish all day.

3. I hope to become an executive one day. The pay is really great once you're at that level.

4. This weekend, I plan on meeting with my friends from college. We're going to go bowling.

5. Next Christmas, I plan to go skiing with my wife and son.

6. I hope to be the top salesman in my division by the end of the year.

7. I want to become the type of person that people can depend on because I enjoy helping others.

8. On my last day of work, I would clean my desk and say goodbye to my colleagues.

9. For my next birthday, I just want to have a quiet evening alone with my wife.

10. In 5 years, I see myself as the head of my division.

1. 다음 휴가때 괌에 가려고 합니다. 바닷물이 매우 깨끗하다고 들었습니다.

2. 은퇴할 자금을 충분히 모았을때 제주도에 집을 하나 사서 하루종일 낚시 할 것입니다.

3. 언젠가 임원이 되고 싶습니다. 그 정도 레벨이 되면 보수가 매우 좋으니까요.

4. 이번 주말 대학교 친구들을 만나기로 하였습니다. 볼링을 치러 가기로 했습니다.

5. 다음 크리스마스에 아내와 아들과 함께 스키를 타러 갈 계획입니다.

6. 올해 말까지 우리 부서에서 최고의 세일즈맨이 되고 싶습니다.

7. 사람들에게 도움을 주는 사람이 되고 싶습니다. 다른사람 돕는 것이 즐거우니깐요.

8. 직장에서의 마지막 날에는 내 책상을 정리하고 동료들에게 작별인사를 할 것입니다.

9. 내 다음 생일에는 아내와 함께 조용한 저녁을 보내고 싶습니다.

10. 5년후의 나의 모습은 우리부서 부서장이 되는 것입니다.

Part 1: Pronunciation

Remember,

SPA Part 1은 모두 발음에 대한 평가가 이루어지는 문항이다
SPA 시험에서 나오는 가장 흔한 발음 실수에 대해서 미리 연습해보자.

Common pronunciation mistakes made on the SPA

F vs P	S vs Sh	B vs V	L vs R	ae vs e	Z vs J
Fan vs pan	Same vs Shame	Ban vs Van	Lan vs Ran	Man vs Men	Zane vs Jane
Fail vs Pale	Said vs Shed	Bane vs Vain	Lane vs Rain	Bad vs Bed	Zed vs Jed
Felt vs Pelt	Sell vs Shell	Bent vs Vent	Lend vs Rend	Fat vs Fet	Zip vs Jip
Fee vs Pea	Seat vs Sheet	Beer vs Veer	Lead vs Reed	Bat vs Bet	Zoo vs Jew
Fear vs Peer	Sip vs Ship	Bill vs Ville	Lift vs Rift	Pan vs Pen	Zoey vs Joey
Fin vs Pin	Sigh vs Shy	Bye vs Vie	Lye vs Rye	Jam vs Gem	
Fine vs Pine	Sought vs Shot	Box vs Vox	Lot vs Rot		
Fought vs Pot	Sore vs Shore	Boat vs Vote	Lore vs Roar		
Four vs Pour	Sun vs Shun		Lust vs Rust		
Fun vs Pun	Sue vs Shoe				

Focus On: Pace / Accent

Pro Tip

The way Koreans stress words is very different from the way native English speakers stress words. In English, it is common to stress two or more consonant sounds in one syllable like caught or change. However, in Korean, sounds are limited to no more than two consonant sounds per syllable.

	English	Correct division	# of syllables	Korean	Syllable division	Syllables
Case 1	change	change	1	체인지	chae-een-gee	3
Case 2	distinct	dis-tinct	2	디스팅트	di-su-ting-tu	4
Case 3	starcraft	star-craft	2	스타크래프트	su-ta-cu-le-pu-tu	6

1 syllable words	2 syllable words	3 syllable words
could	a-cquire	pro-gramm-er
would	air-plane	de-part-ment
should	be-tween	mul-ti-ply
caught	hun-dred	el-e-phant
fought	po-lice	en-ve-lope
bought	moun-tain	un-der-stand
change	e-very	re-co-mmend
raise	dis-cuss	jell-y-fish
praise	bril-liant	a-ppe-tite
speak	a-void	li-brar-y
glove	chal-lenge	sens-i-tive
talk	prac-tice	hon-est-ly
walk	En-glish	ex-pres-sion
shop	A-sia	im-por-tant
film	Eu-rope	ex-pen-sive
card	re-search	A-fri-ca
merge	smart-phone	ad-ven-ture

SPA In-Depth Part 2

Listening Comprehension & Response Technique

Focus on: Accuracy / Response Technique

Question Categories:
 - Personal Narrative
 - Pop Culture
 - Famous People
 - Work Environment
 - Research / Study
 - Technology
 - Transportation
 - Currant Affairs

Part 2: Listening Comprehension & Response Technique

Preview

Q2 Please listen carefully to the following paragraph about a birthday wish and summarize it in your own words, giving as much information from the paragraph as possible. The paragraph can be repeated once.

Next week will be my father's 70th birthday so I want to do something special for him. However, my father keeps insisting that he doesn't want anything big and would simply rather have dinner at his favorite restaurant. My brother wants to respect my father's wish and is planning to just buy him dinner. I on the other hand, am thinking of buying him something nice like a new computer. If I do, I'd be ignoring my father's wish, but I have a feeling that he would like it.

Overview

- Part 2 배점은 32점이다
- 주요 Two segments : 짧은 지문을 듣고 요약하기 / 지문의 토픽에 관한 질문에 대답하기
- Accurancy (Main idea, Details)와 Response Technique (Summary, Opinion)을 채점을 하게된다.
- SPA 시험에서 가장 핵심이고 점수배점이 높은 부분이 바로 Part 2이다. SPA시험은 비즈니스 현장에서의 영어사용 능력을 평가하는 시험이기 때문에 말하기에 있어서 **"이해하고 대답하는 부분"**을 가장 중요하게 생각하고 있다.
- Part 2에서는 문장을 듣고 이해하여 자신의 언어로 요약할 수 있는 능력과 의견을 제시할 수 있어야 한다.

Tip

- 문장을 2번 듣고 핵심적인 내용을 기억해 내는 것이 가장 중요하다.

- 처음 문장을 들을때는 모르는 단어가 나와도 끝까지 일단 들어보도록 한다. 자칫 그 부분 때문에 뒤의 내용을 놓칠 수 있다. 모르는 단어는 2번째 문장 내용을 읽어줄때 평가위원에게 물어보도록 한다.

> 보통 모르는 단어가 Key Point 가 될 수 있으니 넘어가지 말고 평가위원에게 질문하도록 하자.
>
> "I'm not sure what _____ means. Can you explain it please?"

Focus On: Accuracy / Response Technique

Sample

Listening Passage
Next week will be my father's 70th birthday so I want to do something special for him. However, my father keeps insisting that he doesn't want anything big and would simply rather have dinner at his favorite restaurant. My brother wants to respect my father's wish and is planning to just buy him dinner. I on the other hand, am thinking of buying him something nice like a new computer. If I do, I'd be ignoring my father's wish, but I have a feeling that he would like it.

Please summarize what you just heard, giving as much detail as you can.

Summary
The paragraph is about a speaker and his father's birthday wish. It will be his father's 70th birthday soon so he wants to buy him something nice, like a new computer. However, the father insists that the he doesn't want anything more than a dinner at his favorite restaurant. The speaker is not sure if he should ignore his father's wish or buy him something nice.

Follow up
According to the paragraph, the speaker doesn't seem to want to listen to his father's request. If you were in the speaker's position, what would you do?

Response
If I were in the speaker's position, I think I would probably do the same thing because a person's 70th birthday is a big milestone. Even though the father said he just wants a dinner, I don't think he would get upset about getting a nice present.

Follow up
Have you ever had an experience where you bought or received a present that was too nice? What was it and how did you feel?

Response
Yes, I once received an expensive watch from my wife on our anniversary. It was exactly the kind of watch i wanted but I felt bad because all I got for my wife was a photo album with some of our old pictures in it.

리스닝은 하루 아침에 이루어 지지 않는다.
평소에 문장을 듣고 Main Idea를 찾고 세부내용에 대하여 머리속으로 그려보는 훈련을 해야 한다.
미리내 홈페이지 www.mirinaeco.com에서 문장 듣고 연습해 보기.

Part 2: Listening Comprehension & Response Technique

Tip

- 문장 Main Topic의 단서는 평가위원의 첫번째 Direction에서 찾아볼수 있다. 아래의 SPA 평가위원의 첫번째 Direction을 살펴보도록 하자.

Directions: Please listen carefully to **the following paragraph about** a **birthday wish** and summarize it in your own words, giving as much information from the paragraph as possible. The paragraph can be repeated once.

이부분은 시험 시간에 매번 똑같이 읽어주게 되어 있으며 **the following paragraph about** 이후의 부분만 달라지기 때문에 이 부분을 집중해서 들어보면 문장의 Main Idea를 이해할 수 있다. 아래 예시의 경우는 **birthday wish** 에 관련된 토픽임을 알 수 있다.

듣기 문장을 2번듣고 요약하기란 처음 만나면 당황하기 쉬운 부분이다.

평소에 듣기 지문을 많이 듣고 아래와 같은 방법으로 Detail, Keyword를 찾는 연습이 필요하다.

Listening Passage

Next week will be **my father's 70th birthday** [detail] so I want to do something special for him. However, my father keeps **insisting** [key word] that **he doesn't want anything big** [detail] and **would simply rather have dinner at his favorite restaurant** [detail]. My brother wants to respect my father's wish and is planning to just buy him dinner. I on the other hand, am **thinking of buying him something nice like a new computer** [detail]. If I do, I'd be **ignoring** [key word] my father's wish, but I have a feeling that he would like it.

Note

- 요약하기에 훌륭한 포맷은 문장의 Main Idea로 시작하는 요약이다.
  그 다음에 2~3개의 문장의 세부사항을 포함하여 말하고 (키워드를 더 추가하여 말하면 좋다),
  마지막으로 추론하여 나온 나의 의견을 제시하여 요약을 마무리하는 것이 BEST 답변이다.

- 문장을 요약해서 대답할 때는 아래 내용을 반드시 포함하도록 한다.
  - main idea
  - specific details (2-3)
  - key words
  - an inference about the passage or a simple conclusion about the passage.

Hint: 답변자의 요약 내용에 따라 평가위원은 내용 이해도를 확인하기 위한 추가질문이 이루어 질 수 있다.

Summary:

Intro   The paragraph is about a speaker and his father's birthday wish.

Detail 1   It will be his father's 70th birthday soon so

Detail 2   he wants to buy him something nice, like a new computer.

Detail 3   However, the father insists that the he doesn't want anything more than a dinner at his favorite restaurant.

Inference   The speaker is not sure if he should ignore his father's wish or buy him something nice.

Practice making your own summary by providing an intro, 3 details, and an inference about the listening paragraph.

Intro   ....

Detail 1   ....

Detail 2   ....

Detail 3   ....

Inference   ....

Part 2: Listening Comprehension & Response Technique

Pro Tip

Follow Up Questions:

- 요약하기를 끝내면 듣기 문장에 관련된 추가 질문이 이어지게 된다. 보통 토픽과 관련된 당신의 경험 이라든지 "만약에 당신이라면 어떻게 하겠는가" 라는 질문이 주어진다.

- 첫번째 추가질문 이후 남은 시험 시간과 답변에 따라 평가위원은 1개의 추가질문을 더 결정할 수 있다. 추가질문 역시 4개 유형의 질문중의 하나가 나올 것이다.

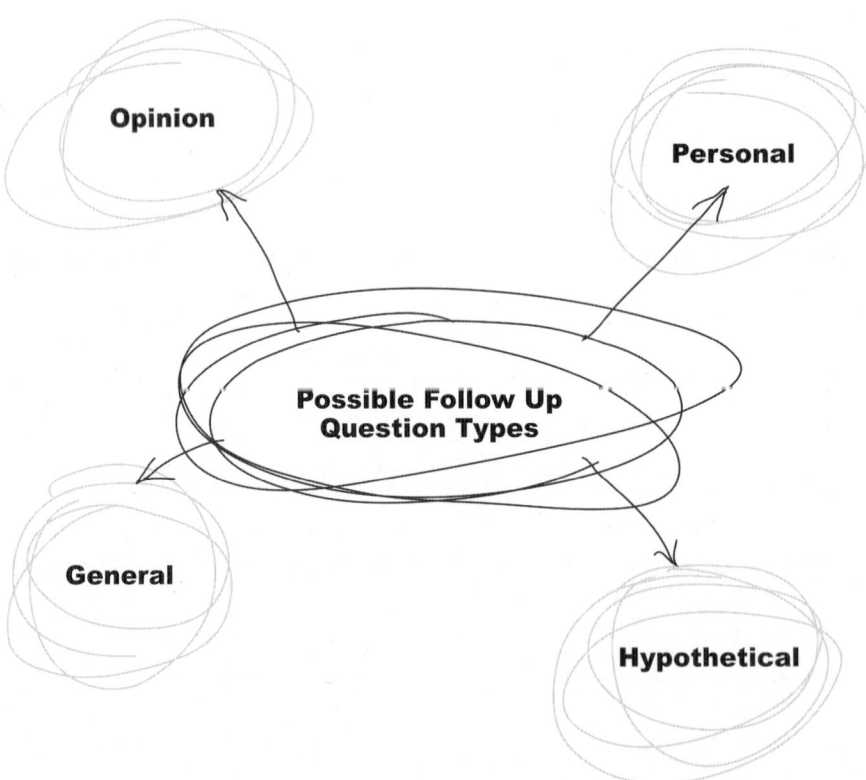

Focus On: Accuracy / Response Technique

Possible Follow Up Questions

Case 1: Opinion	Do you think the speaker should listen to his father's wish or ignore it and buy him something nice?
Case 2: Personal	Have you ever had an experience where you bought or received a present that was too nice? What was it and how did you feel?
Case 3: General	What are some popular gifts to buy for parents?
Case 4: Hypothetical	If you were in the speaker's position, what would you do?

Follow Up #1 According to the paragraph, the speaker doesn't seem to want to listen to his father's request. If you were in the speaker's position, what would you do?
문장에서 화자는 아버지의 요청을 들어주고 싶어하지 않는 것 같습니다.
만약 당신이 화자의 입장이라면 어떻게 할 것 같습니까?

Response If I were in the speaker's position, I think I would probably do the same thing because a person's 70th birthday is a big milestone. Even though the father said he just wants a dinner, I don't think he would get upset about getting a nice present.
만약에 제가 화자의 입장이라면 저 역시 화자랑 똑같이 행동했을 것 같습니다. 왜냐하면 70번째 생일은 한 개인의 커다란 이정표이기 때문입니다. 아버지가 저녁만 먹자고 했더라도 제가 좋은 선물을 선물해드려도 기분 나빠하지는 않을 것 같습니다.

Follow Up #2 Have you ever had an experience where you bought or received a present that was too nice? What was it and how did you feel?
값진 선물을 사거나 받아본 경험이 있습니까? 무엇이었으며 어떤 느낌이었습니까?

Response Yes, I once received an expensive watch from my wife on our anniversary. It was exactly the kind of watch i wanted but I felt bad because all I got for my wife was a photo album with some of our old pictures in it.
네. 아내가 결혼기념일에 비싼 시계를 선물해 주었어요. 제가 원했던 종류의 시계였지만 기분은 좋지 않았어요. 왜냐하면 저는 아내에게 옛날 사진을 집어 넣은 앨범을 선물해주었거든요.

Part 2: Listening Comprehension & Response Technique
Personal Narrative

Personal Narrative(개인의 이야기) 지문은 딜레마를 갖고 있는 어떤 화자의 이야기로 구성되어 있다.

Example passage:

Please listen carefully to the following paragraph about finding a job and summarize it in your own words, giving as much information from the paragaph as possible. The paragraph can be repeated once.

After graduating from college, I had difficulty finding a good job. It was very frustrating because I had worked hard to get good grades and graduate from one of the best schools in my country. Whenever I interviewed for a job, I was always turned down because I didn't have enough qualified experience. It was extremely unfair because I couldn't get any experience without having experience already.

Please summarize what you just heard in your own words, giving as much detail as possible.

Intro ....

Detail 1 ....

Detail 2 ....

Detail 3 ....

Inference ....

Focus On: Accuracy / Response Technique

Personal Narrative

Possible follow up question to the listening passage:

Case 1: Opinion — According to the paragraph, the speaker had difficulty finding a job after graduating from college. In your opinion, what could the speaker do to improve his chances of getting a job?

Case 2: Personal — According to the paragraph, the speaker had difficulty finding a job after graduating from college. How was your job search after graduating from college?

Case 3: General — According to the paragraph, the speaker had difficulty finding a job after graduating from college. Is this a common problem for recent college graduates in your country?

Case 4: Hypothetical — According to the paragraph, the speaker had difficulty finding a job after graduating from college. What would you have done if you were in the speaker's position?

Personal Narrative

After graduating from college, I had difficulty finding a good job. It was very frustrating because I had worked hard to get good grades and graduate from one of the best schools in my country. Whenever I interviewed for a job, I was always turned down because I didn't have enough qualified experience. It was extremely unfair because I couldn't get any experience without having experience.

Case 1: Opinion

In your opinion, what could the speaker do to improve his chances of getting a job?

The speaker could improve his chances of getting a job by looking for internships. The pay won't be as high at first, but it will make it easier for him to get into a company that he wants to work for. Once he builds experience through the internship, he can apply for other positions.

Case 2: Personal

How was your job search after graduating from college?

My experience was complicated. After graduating, I applied for many jobs within my field of study but was not accepted into any position that I wanted. I eventually found a nice job in a field I originally did not consider. Having an open mind helped me to find a job quickly so perhaps other people looking for jobs should do the same.

Case 3: General

The speaker had difficulty finding a job after graduating from college. Is this a common problem for recent college graduates in your country?

It wasn't a problem in the past but recently, it is a very common problem. I think as time goes by, college degrees are becoming more and more common so it is getting harder for recent graduates in Korea to find good jobs out of college.

Case 4: Hypothetical

What would you have done if you were in the speaker's position?

If I were in the speaker's position, I would have looked for a part-time job. It would allow me to have time to still look for the job that I want while at the same time, build my experience as well as earn me a little money.

Focus On: Accuracy / Response Technique

Personal Narrative

대학을 졸업하고 좋은 직장을 찾는데 어려움을 겪었었다. 우리나라에서 가장 좋은 학교를 졸업하고 좋은 성적을 얻기위해 노력했었는데 너무 좌절감을 느꼈었다. 직장 면접을 볼때마다 항상 거절당했었다. 왜냐하면 나는 경력이 없었기 때문이다. 그것은 정말 끔찍하게 불공평했다. 직장경험을 갖지 않았기 때문에 당연히 경력을 쌓을수가 없기 때문이다.

Case 1: Opinion

당신 생각에는 화자가 직업을 찾을수 있는 기회를 향상시키기 위해서 해야 할 것은 무엇인것 같습니까?

화자는 인턴쉽을 찾아 봄으로서 직업을 찾는 기회를 향상시킬 수 있습니다. 임금은 처음에 높지는 않지만 일하고 싶은 곳에 쉽게 들어갈 수 있을 것입니다. 인턴쉽으로 경험을 쌓으면 다른 포지션에도 지원할 수 있습니다.

Case 2: Personal

학교를 졸업 후 구직중이었던 당신의 경험은 어땠습니까?

저의 경험은 복잡했습니다. 졸업후에 제가 공부했던 분야의 직업에 많은 이력서를 냈지만 제가 원하는 분야 어디에서도 합격을 받지 못했습니다.
저는 결국 제가 고려하지 않았던 분야에서 좋은 직장을 찾게되었습니다.
열린 마음으로 직업을 찾으면 빨리 찾을 수 있는 것 같습니다. 아마도 다른 사람들도 열린마음으로 직업을 찾으면 빨리 찾을 수 있을거라 생각합니다.

Case 3: General

화자는 대학 졸업후에 직장 찾는데 어려움을 겪었습니다. 당신의 나라에서 최근 대학을 졸업한 학생들에게 흔히 일어나는 문제인가요?

과거에는 문제가 아니었으나 최근에는 흔한 문제가 되었습니다. 제 생각에는 시간이 흘러 대학교 학위받은 사람들이 더 많아지고 있기 때문에 최근 대학을 졸업한 사람에게는 좋은 직장을 찾기가 더 더욱 어려워 지고 있습니다.

Case 4: Hypothetical

당신이 화자의 상황이라면 무엇을 했을까요?

제가 만약 화자의 위치라면 아르바이트를 찾아 보았을 것입니다.
똑같은 시간에 여전히 내가 원하는 직업을 찾아 볼 수 있으면서 경험을 쌓고 약간의 돈도 벌 수 있기 때문입니다.

Part 2: Listening Comprehension & Response Technique
Pop Culture

대중 문화 지문은 보통 현재 인기있는 트렌드의 주제로 시작된다.
트렌드를 어느정도 설명한 이후 트렌드가 주는 사회 영향에 초점이 되어 이야기가 진행된다.

Example passage:

Please listen carefully to the following paragraph about Hollywood and summarize it in your own words, giving as much information from the paragaph as possible. The paragraph can be repeated once.

Hollywood has long been a place where tourists go to take pictures of famous movie stars and characters. Many locals like to wear costumes of popular movie characters and walk the streets, looking for tourists to take pictures with. However, many tourists do not realize that these people aren't taking pictures for free. After taking a picture with tourists, many of these costumed people will demand a fee for their picture taking services which can often cost up to $20 a picture.

Please summarize what you just heard in your own words, giving as much detail as possible.

Intro ....

Detail 1 ....

Detail 2 ....

Detail 3 ....

Inference ....

Focus On: Accuracy / Response Technique

Pop Culture

Possible follow up question to the listening passage:

Case 1: According to the paragraph, people wearing costumes in Hollywood often demand a fee for having their picture taken. Do you think it's fair for these costumed individuals to charge a fee for having a picture taken with them?
Opinion

....

....

Case 2: According to the paragraph, many tourists do not realize the costumed people in Hollywood demand a fee. Have you ever been in a situation where you were suddenly charged an unexpected fee? If not, how would you react if you were?
Personal

....

....

Case 3: According to the paragraph, many tourists do not realize the costumed people in Hollywood demand a fee. If a tourist is tricked into a scam while traveling, is it the tourist's fault for not knowing local practices?
General

....

....

Case 4: According to the paragraph, many tourists do not realize the costumed people in Hollywood demand a fee. If you were a tourist taking pictures, how would you feel if someone suddenly asked you to pay for the pictures you just took?
Hypothetical

....

....

Pop Culture

Hollywood has long been a place where tourists go to take pictures of famous movie characters. Many locals like to wear costumes of popular movie characters and walk the streets, looking for tourists to take pictures with. However, a lot of tourists do not realize that these people aren't taking pictures free. After taking a picture with tourists, many of these costumed individuals will demand a fee for their picture taking services which can often cost up to $20 a picture.

Case 1: Opinion

Do you think it's fair for these costumed individuals to charge a fee for having a picture taken with them?

I think it's fair. They are providing a service so I think they have a right to charge a fee. However, to prevent any surprises, they should probably make it clear to the tourists that they charge a fee to have their picture taken.

Case 2: Personal

Have you ever been in a situation where you were suddenly charged an unexpected fee? If not, how would you react if you were?

Yes, once when I was visiting the United States, I took a taxi from the airport to my hotel room. I knew there was a tip for restaurant servers in America, but I didn't know about tipping taxi drivers. I tried to go to the hotel lobby without giving a tip to the taxi driver and he became very upset. I felt embarrassed for not knowing and apologized to the driver.

Case 3: General

If a tourist is tricked into a scam while traveling, is it the tourist's fault for not knowing local practices?

I think these days, it is mostly the tourist's fault for not knowing local practices better. There is a wealth of information on the internet for travelers to research before traveling to a certain area. If you spend some time studying about the area you plan to visit, I think you can avoid a lot of trouble.

Case 4: Hypothetical

If you were a tourist taking pictures, how would you feel if someone suddenly asked you to pay for the pictures you just took?

I think if the person didn't mention anything about money before I took the pictures, I would be a little upset. In most countries that I've been to, people who wear costumes usually never ask for money after you take their picture so normally, I wouldn't assume I'd have to pay. If they made it clear that I had to pay before I took the picture, then I would simply not take it.

Focus On: Accuracy / Response Technique

Pop Culture

헐리우드는 유명한 영화 캐릭터들과 함께 사진 찍는 오래된 장소이다. 많은 지역 주민들이 유명한 영화배우 캐릭터 복장을 입고 거리를 돌아다니며 관광객들과 함께 사진을 찍어줍니다. 그러나 많은 관광객들이 함께 사진 찍는 것이 무료가 아니라는 것을 알아차리지 못합니다. 캐릭터 복장을 입은 사람들이 관광객들과 사진 찍은 후 사진 찍은 비용을 지불하라고 요구한다고 합니다. 보통 가격은 사진당 20$까지 요구하기도 합니다.

Case 1: Opinion

이러한 의상을 입은 사람들이 그들과 함께 찍은 사진을 가지고 비용을 요구 하는 것이 괜찮다고 생각하십니까?

제 생각에는 괜찮은 것 같습니다. 그 사람들은 서비스를 제공하는 것이고 거기에 대한 수수료를 요구하는 것이라고 생각합니다. 그러나 논란을 피하기 위해서 그들은 관광객들에게 사진을 찍으면 돈을 내야 한다고 명확하게 밝혀야 합니다.

Case 2: Personal

당신은 예상하지 못한 곳에서 돈을 요구당한 이러한 경험이 있습니까? 만약 그런 경험이 없다면 이럴 경우 어떻게 행동하시겠습니까?

네, 미국에 한번 갔을때 공항에서 호텔까지 택시를 탔습니다. 미국에서는 레스토랑에서 팁을 주는 것은 알고 있었지만 택시 운전기사에게도 주는 것은 몰랐습니다. 운전기사에게 팁을 주지않고 내리려고 하자 운전기사는 매우 화냈고 나는 팁을 주는 것을 몰라 당황했고 곧 택시 운전기사에게 사과를 했습니다.

Case 3: General

관광객이 여행중에 사기에 속은 경우, 현지 관행을 이해하지 못한 관광객의 잘못 이라고 생각합니까?

제 생각에는 오늘날에 관광객이 현지 관행을 모르는 것은 대부분이 관광객의 잘못이라고 생각합니다. 여행자가 특정지역을 여행하기 전에 인터넷에서 현지의 풍부한 정보를 미리 찾아볼 수 있습니다. 여행하기로 계획한 지역에 약간의 시간을 투자하여 공부하면 많은 불편함을 피할 수 있을거라 생각합니다.

Case 4: Hypothetical

만약 당신이 사신을 씪는 관광객이었고 누군가 갑자기 사진 찍은것에 대해 돈을 내라고 요구하면 어떠할 것 같습니까?

만약에 사진찍기 전에 아무런 이야기를 해주지 않았다면 화가 났을 것이다. 지금껏 다녀 본 대부분의 나라에서는 코스튬을 입은 사람들은 사진찍은 이후에 돈을 요구하지 않았기 때문에 돈을 지불해야 한다고 생각해보지 않았습니다. 만약에 사진찍기 전에 돈을 지불해야 한다고 미리 알려준다면 저는 쉽게 사진을 찍지는 않을 것 같습니다.

Part 2: Listening Comprehension & Response Technique
Famous People

유명인사 지문은 보통 사회적으로 많이 알려져 있는 사람에 대한 이야기이다
지문은 유명인사의 주요 업적에 대해 이야기 할 것이고 오늘날 사람들이 그 사람을 어떻게 평가하는지에 대한 이야기로 끝이난다.

Example passage:

Please listen carefully to the following paragraph about Michael Jackson and summarize it in your own words, giving as much information from the paragaph as possible. The paragraph can be repeated once.

Michael Jackson, also known as the King of Pop, was a famous American singer and global icon. He started his career when he was six years old as a member of the Jackson 5. After spending his childhood as the lead singer for his group, he began his solo career in 1971. He would go on to become one of the most successful musicians throughout history. His album Thriller is still the best selling album of all time.

Please summarize what you just heard in your own words, giving as much detail as possible.

Intro ....

Detail 1 ....

Detail 2 ....

Detail 3 ....

Inference ....

Focus On: Accuracy / Response Technique

Famous People

Possible follow up question to the listening passage:

Case 1:
Opinion

According to the paragraph, Michael Jackson was one of the most famous singers in the world. In your opinion, what are some advantages and disadvantages of being famous?

....

....

Case 2:
Personal

According to the paragraph, Michael Jackson was one of the most famous singers in the world. Would you want to become a famous person? Why or why not?

....

....

Case 3:
General

According to the paragraph, Michael Jackson started his career at the age of 6. What is the typical age when people start working in your country? Do you think this is too early or too late?

....

....

Case 4:
Hypothetical

According to the paragraph, Michael Jackson was one of the most famous singers in the world. If you were as famous as Michael Jackson, what would you do?

....

....

Famous People

Michael Jackson, also known as the King of Pop, was a famous American singer and global icon. He started his career when he was six years old as a member of the Jackson 5. After spending his childhood as the lead singer for his group, he began his solo career in 1971. He would go on to become one of the most successful musicians throughout history. His album Thriller is still the best selling album of all time.

Case 1: Opinion

According to the paragraph, Michael Jackson was one of the most famous singers in the world. In your opinion, what are some advantages and disadvantages of being famous?

I think an advantage of being famous is that what you say or do becomes more meaningful because it reaches more people; your opinions have a significant impact. A disadvantage of being famous is the lack of privacy. I think it would be very difficult to live comfortably if people are always watching you.

Case 2: Personal

According to the paragraph, Michael Jackson was one of the most famous singers in the world. Would you want to become a famous person? Why or why not?

Yes, I think I would want to become famous. The reason why is because I think it would make it a lot easier for me to make money. All you have to do is make a lot of commercials. For example, Kim Yuna used her fame to earn a lot of money from HomePlus commercials.

Case 3: General

According to the paragraph, Michael Jackson started his career at the age of 6. What is the typical age when people start working in your country? Do you think this is too early or too late?

I think most people in Korea start to work in their mid twenties. For men, it's a little later because of military service. I think the starting age is a little high compared to other countries. Unfortunately, in Korea, young people are too busy with their studies to work part-time or start their careers earlier.

Case 4: Hypothetical

According to the paragraph, Michael Jackson was one of the most famous singers in the world. If you were as famous as Michael Jackson, what would you do?

If I were as famous as Michael Jackson, I would probably look for a more private home to live in. If I remember correctly, Michael Jackson lived in a very secluded ranch called Neverland. I think I would try to look for a house that's similar because I don't think I would be able to tolerate all the paparazzi.

Focus On: Accuracy / Response Technique

Famous People

팝의 황제로 유명한 마이클 잭슨은 유명한 미국의 가수이며 글로벌 아이콘이었다. 마이클 잭슨은 6살때 Jackson 5 의 멤버로 데뷔를 하였다. 그의 그룹에서 리드 싱어로 유년기를 보낸후에 1971년에 솔로 활동을 시작하였다. 그는 역사상 가장 성공한 뮤지션으로 명성을 날리게 되었다. 그의 앨범 "Thriller"는 여전히 베스트 셀러 앨범으로 남았다.

Case 1: Opinion

문장에 따르면, 마이클잭슨은 세계에서 가장 유명한 가수중의 한명이었다고 한다. 당신 생각에 유명인사가 되는 것의 장단점은 무엇이라고 생각합니까?

제 생각에는 유명인사가 되는 것의 장점은 당신이 말하고 행동하는 것들의 의미가 대중에게 전달되어 지는 것입니다. 그렇기 때문에 당신의 의견에 중요한 영향력이 실리게 됩니다. 유명인사가 되는 것의 단점은 사생활이 제한된다는 것입니다. 사람들이 항상 당신을 바라보고 있으면 편안하게 살기가 어려울 것 같습니다.

Case 2: Personal

문장에 따르면, 마이클 잭슨은 세계에서 가장 유명한 가수 중의 한 명이었다고 한다. 당신은 유명인사가 되고 싶습니까? 그 이유는?

네. 저도 유명한 사람이 되고 싶습니다. 이유는 돈을 벌기 쉬워지니까요. 해야 할 일이라곤 어떤 물건에 대해 광고만 하면 되니깐요. 예를 들어 김연아가 자신의 명성을 이용해 홈플러스 광고를 찍었고 많은 돈을 벌었습니다.

Case 3: General

문장에 따르면, 마이클 잭슨은 6살때 데뷔를 하여 일을 하기 시작했습니다. 당신의 나라에서는 보통 몇살에 사람들이 일을 시작합니까? 당신 생각에 그 나이가 너무 이른가요? 늦은가요?

제 생각에 대부분의 한국사람들은 20대 중반에 일을 시작하는 것 같습니다. 남자의 경우는 군대를 갔다오기 때문에 조금 더 늦게 시작합니다. 다른 나라와 비교하면 조금 늦을 수도 있지만 한국에서는 어렸을때는 공부하기에 너무 바빠 아르바이트나 일을 시작하기 어렵습니다.

Case 4: Hypothetical

문장에 따르면, 마이클 잭슨은 세계에서 가장 유명한 가수 중의 한 명이었다고 한다. 만약에 당신이 마이클 잭슨 처럼 유명하다면 무엇을 하겠습니까?

만약에 내가 마이클 잭슨처럼 유명하다면, 아마도 좀 더 사생활을 지킬 수 있는 집에서 살 것 같습니다. 내 기억이 맞다면, 마이클 잭슨은 "네버랜드" 라고 불리우는 외딴 목장에서 살았습니다. 아마 저 역시 네버랜드 같은 비슷한 집을 찾아서 살 것 같습니다. 왜냐하면 파파라치 같은 사람들을 피하고 싶기 때문입니다.

Work Environment

업무환경 지문은 일반적인 업무에 관련된 이슈에 대한 이야기를 다룬다.

Example passage:

Please listen carefully to the following paragraph about missing work and summarize it in your own words, giving as much information from the paragaph as possible. The paragraph can be repeated once.

Employees taking days off of work can cost companies a lot of time, production, and ultimately money. Many companies try to limit the amount of days missed by employees, including sick days and personal holidays. In addition, most companies these days are requiring employees to provide proof as to why they missed work such as a medical bill or a doctor's note. Not providing proof is often enough to get the employee fired from the company.

Please summarize what you just heard in your own words, giving as much detail as possible.

Intro ....

Detail 1 ....

Detail 2 ....

Detail 3 ....

Inference ....

Focus On: Accuracy / Response Technique
Work Environment

Possible follow up question to the listening passage:

Case 1: According to the paragraph, many companies require their employees to
Opinion provide proof for missing work. What is your opinion of this?

....

....

Case 2: According to the paragraph, many companies require their employees to
Personal provide proof for missing work. Does your company require you to provide
some sort of proof for missing work? How do you feel about your company's
policy?

....

....

Case 3: According to the paragraph, many companies are trying to reduce the
General amount of days missed by their employees. Do employees in your country
get enough days off from work?

....

....

Case 4: According to the paragraph, many employers require their employees to
Hypothetical provide proof for missing work. If you were the boss and an employee
missed work without providing valid proof to show why he missed work,
what would you do?

....

....

Work Environment

Employees taking days off of work can cost companies a lot of time, production, and ultimately money. Many companies try to limit the amount of days missed by employees, including sick days and personal holidays. In addition, most companies these days are requiring employees to provide proof as to why they missed work such as a medical bill or a doctor's note. Not providing proof is often enough cause to lead to termination from the company.

Case 1: Opinion

According to the paragraph, many companies require their employees to provide proof for missing work. What is your opinion of this?

I think it is a fair policy. If you really have a valid reason for missing work, there shouldn't be any difficulty in getting proof. I like that it deters people from lying about missing work and I think as long as the company enforces the same rule for everyone equally, it is a very reasonable policy.

Case 2: Personal

Does your company require you to provide some sort of proof for missing work? How do you feel about your company's policy?

Yes, my company requires me to bring in valid proof if I miss work. I feel like it is unnecessary and just makes it a bigger hassle to miss work. Sometimes, when I feel very ill, I prefer to just stay home and rest rather than visit a hospital. With this policy however, I am forced to go to the hospital just to get a receipt showing medical proof. My company should just trust their employees.

Case 3: General

Do employees in your country get enough days off from work?

No, people in my country do not get enough days off work. Most people go to work, even when they are sick. I hear about workers in places like Norway and Sweden where they get months off at a time and I realize people in my country work way too much. Taking even a few weeks off is difficult at some companies in my country.

Case 4: Hypothetical

If you were a boss and one of your employees missed work without bringing in valid proof for missing work, what would you do?

I would ask that person why they missed work. If it sounds like they had a good reason, I will let him off the hook just once. If he does it again, however, I would have to fire him.

Work Environment

Focus On: Accuracy / Response Technique

임직원들이 휴가를 사용하는 것은 회사로서는 많은 시간, 생산 그리고 궁극적으로 돈을 소비할 수가 있다. 많은 회사들이 임직원들의 병가라던지 개인휴가 같은 회사에서 쉬는 날의 총 일수를 제한하려 하고 있다 더불어 대부분의 회사들은 임직원들이 회사에 빠지게 되면 병원비 영수증이나 진단서등을 제출하도록 하고 있다. 이러한 증빙 서류를 제출하지 않으면 종종 회사를 떠나야 할 때도 생긴다.

Case 1: Opinion

문장에 따르면, 많은 회사들이 자신의 임직원들이 업무에 빠지게 될 경우 결근 증빙서류를 제출하도록 하는데 이것에 대해 어떻게 생각하십니까?

정단한 정책인 것 같습니다. 결근한 정당한 사유가 있다면 증빙 자료를 제출하는 것은 문제가 없을것이라고 생각합니다. 거짓말로 결근하는 사람이 사라지지 않는 한 회사가 모든 사람에게 똑같이 정책을 적용할 것이라고 생각하며 이는 매우 합리적인 정책이라고 생각합니다.

Case 2: Personal

당신의 회사도 결근을 하게 될 경우 증빙자료를 제출하도록 합니까? 이러한 회사 정책에 대해서 어떻게 생각합니까?

네, 우리 회사도 결근시에 증빙서류를 제출하도록 합니다. 저는 이러한 것이 불필요하다고 생각하고 결근 하는 것에 대해 굉장히 귀찮게 만드는 것 같습니다. 때때로 매우 아프거나 하게 되면 병원가는 것보다 집에서 쉬고 싶을때가 있습니다. 이러한 정책때문에 억지로 병원에가서 진단서를 받아야 할때도 있습니다. 회사는 직원을 신뢰해야 한다고 생각합니다.

Case 3: General

당신의 나라에서는 임직원들이 충분한 휴가를 얻고 있습니까?

아니요. 우리나라에서는 충분한 휴가를 얻고 있지 못하고 있습니다. 대부분의 사람들은 몸이 아프더라도 회사에 나갑니다. 노르웨이나 스웨덴같은 나라는 한 번에 한 달씩 쉴 수 있다고 들었는데 우리나라 사람들은 일을 너무 많이 한다는 걸 알게 되었습니다. 우리나라에서의 어떤 회사에서는 단 몇주 쉬는 것도 어려운 실정입니다.

Case 4: Hypothetical

만약에 당신이 회사의 사장이고 당신의 직원이 증빙서류 없이 회사를 결근 했다면 당신은 어떻게 하겠습니까?

결근 사유에 대해서 물어볼 것입니다. 만약에 근거가 충분하다면 한 번 넘어갈 수 있습니다. 그러나 다시 또 그런다면 해고를 할 것 같습니다.

Part 2: Listening Comprehension & Response Technique

Research / Study

연구 조사 지문은 최신 연구 결과 요약을 중심으로 내용을 전개해 나갈 것이다.

Example passage:

Please listen carefully to the following paragraph about popular songs and summarize it in your own words, giving as much information from the paragaph as possible. The paragraph can be repeated once.

A study carried out by the University of Southern California has revealed that songs that have a repetitive chorus are more likely to become a success than songs that have varied sounds. Analysing the top songs from the past 70 years, the researchers found that the most popular songs all generally have an easy to remember chorus that keeps repeating throughout the song. They found that the more repetitive the song, the more popular it was. According to the researchers, it is because repetitive songs put less strain on the brain.

Please summarize what you just heard in your own words, giving as much detail as possible.

Intro ....

Detail 1 ....

Detail 2 ....

Detail 3 ....

Inference ....

Focus On: Accuracy / Response Technique
Research / Study

Possible follow up question to the listening passage:

Case 1: According to the paragraph, repetitive songs are more popular than
Opinion non-repetitive songs. What are your thoughts on this?

....

....

Case 2: According to the paragraph, repetitive songs are more popular than
Personal non-repetitive songs. What are some of your favorite songs? Are they
repetitive songs?

....

....

Case 3: According to the paragraph, repetitive songs are more popular than
General non-repetitive songs. What are some popular songs in Korea. Are
they repetitive?

....

....

Case 4: According to the paragraph, repetitive songs are more popular than
Hypothetical non-repetitive songs. If you had to listen to one song over and over
again, which song would you choose and why?

....

....

Part 2: Listening Comprehension & Response Technique

Research / Study

A study carried out by the University of Southern California has revealed that songs that have a repetitive chorus are more likely to become a success than songs that have varied sounds. Analysing the top songs from the past 70 years, the researchers found that the most popular songs all generally have an easy to remember chorus that keeps repeating throughout the song. They found that the more repetitive the song, the more popular it was. According to the researchers, it is because repetitive songs put less strain on the brain.

Case 1: Opinion

According to the paragraph, repetitive songs are more popular than non-repetitive songs. What are your thoughts on this?

I think it makes sense. Repetitive songs are easier to listen to and much easier to remember. If I think about all my favorite songs, I only really think about the chorus. That's usually the only part of the song that I care about, and I think most people are similar to me in that regard.

Case 2: Personal

What are some of your favorite songs? Are they repetitive songs?

Some of my favorite songs include "Yesterday" by the Beatles, "Good Riddance" by Green Day, and "Gee" by Girls Generation. I never really thought about it until now but after hearing the passage, I realize that they're all repetitive songs with a catchy chorus.

Case 3: General

What are some popular songs in Korea. Are they repetitive?

Some popular songs in Korea include Psy's "Gangnam Style", Crayon Pop's "Jumping", and APink's "Love L.U.V.". The chorus for these songs are all very repetitive but at the same time, very catchy. If you sing just a small part of the chorus, everyone in Korea will recognize the song.

Case 4: Hypothetical

If you had to listen to one song over and over again, which song would you choose and why?

If I had to choose one song to listen to over and over again, it would be "Up and Down" by EXID. When I first heard that song, I listened to it over and over again for a few days. I really like their upbeat tune and simple chorus. It's very easy to listen to.

Focus On: Accuracy / Response Technique

Research / Study

남가주대학의 연구조사에 의하면 반복적인 코러스가 있는 음악이 다양한 사운드를 가진 음악보다 성공할 가능성이 더 높다고 한다. 과거 70년동안의 인기 음악들을 분석해보면 가장 인기있는 음악들은 모두 일반적으로 음악 속에서 기억하기 쉬운 코러스가 반복되고 있었다. 또한 반복적인 음악들이 더 유명해지는 것으로 조사되었다. 연구조사원들에 따르면 반복적인 음악들은 뇌에 부담을 덜 주기 때문이라고 한다.

Case 1: Opinion

문장에 따르면 반복적인 음악들이 일반적인 음악보다 더 인기가 있다고 한다. 이 연구조사에 대해 어떻게 생각하는가?

맞는 논리인것 같습니다. 반복적인 음악들은 듣기 쉽고 기억하기도 쉽습니다. 제가 좋아하는 음악들도 코러스만 기억이 나는것 같습니다. 일반적으로 음악을 들을때 관심을 두며 듣는 부분이고 대부분의 사람들도 그 부분에 있어서 비슷할 것이라 생각합니다.

Case 2: Personal

당신이 좋아하는 음악은 무엇인가요? 반복적인 음악인가요?

내가 좋아하는 음악은 비틀즈의 "Yesterday", 그린데이의 "Good Riddance", 소녀시대의 "Gee" 입니다.. 지금까지 이 음악들의 인기비결을 생각해 본 적 없었는데 문장을 듣고 생각해보니 내가 좋아하는 이 노래들도 반복적인 노래이며 기억하기 쉬운 노래들이라는 것을 알게 되었습니다.

Case 3: General

한국에서 유명한 음악은 무엇인가요? 반복적인 음악인가요?

한국에서 유명한 싸이의 "강남스타일", 크레용팝의 "점핑", 에이핑크의 "Love L.U.V" 노래의 코러스를 들어보면 모두 매우 반복적인 노래입니다. 또한 매우 쉽게 들을 수 있는 음악들입니다. 만약에 당신이 코러스의 한부분만 불러보더라도 한국의 대부분의 사람들이 알아차릴 수 있을것입니다.

Case 4: Hypothetical

만약에 당신이 한 음악을 반복해서 듣는다면 어떤 노래를 고를 것 같습니까? 이유는요?

만약에 반복해서 들을 노래를 고르라고 한다면 EXID의 "위아래"를 선택할 것 같습니다. 몇 일 반복해서 들어보니 신나는 리듬과 심플한 코러스가 마음에 들었습니다. 정말 쉽게 들을 수 있는 음악입니다.

Part 2: Listening Comprehension & Response Technique

Technology

기술에 관련된 토픽 지문은 현재 최신 기술 발명품이나 트렌드, 혁신적인 것들에 대해 아웃라인을 그리면서 이야기를 풀어나간다.

Example passage:

Please listen carefully to the following paragraph about a new cosmetic procedure and summarize it in your own words, giving as much information from the paragaph as possible. The paragraph can be repeated once.

A new cosmetic procedure has been developed that permanently changes brown eyes into blue eyes. The procedure, which takes only 20 seconds will cost around $5,000. While the procedure is still undergoing long term safety testing in the United States, 17 patients in Mexico and 20 in Costa Rica have already undergone the treatment with no major complications. The developers expect it to clear government safety regulations soon and for it to be available to the general public shortly.

Please summarize what you just heard in your own words, giving as much detail as possible.

Intro ....

Detail 1 ....

Detail 2 ....

Detail 3 ....

Inference ....

Focus On: Accuracy / Response Technique

Technology

Possible follow up question to the listening passage:

Case 1:
Opinion

According to the paragraph, a new procedure can change brown eyes into blue eyes. What is your opinion of cosmetic procedures?

....

....

Case 2:
Personal

According to the paragraph, a new procedure can change brown eyes into blue eyes. Would you ever consider undergoing an experimental procedure?

....

....

Case 3:
General

According to the paragraph, several people have already undergone the eye color change procedure. What are the benefits of changing your eye color?

....

....

Case 4:
Hypothetical

According to the paragraph, a new procedure can change brown eyes into blue eyes. If you could change your eye color to any color that you wanted, what color would it be and why?

....

....

Technology

A new cosmetic procedure has been developed that permanently changes brown eyes into blue eyes. The procedure, which takes only 20 seconds will cost around $5,000. While the procedure is still undergoing long term safety testing in the United States, 17 patients in Mexico and 20 in Costa Rica have already undergone the treatment with no major complications. The developers expect it to clear government safety regulations soon and for it to be available to the general public shortly.

Case 1: **What is your opinion of cosmetic procedures?**
Opinion

I think it's a wonderful technology and we are blessed to have this sort of modern convenience available to us. Cosmetic procedures these days are quite safe compared to in the past and costs a lot less as well. I think that is one of the reasons why so many people in Korea undergo cosmetic surgery.

Case 2: **Would you ever consider undergoing an experimental procedure?**
Personal

Under normal circumstances, I would not consider undergoing any sort of experimental procedure because I don't want to risk putting my health in danger. However, if I had a severe illness and there was an experimental procedure that could cure me, then I might consider it.

Case 3: **What are the benefits of changing your eye color?**
General

If you change your eye color, you will most likely stand out more. This is especially true for Koreans because normally, all Koreans have brown eyes. If there was a Korean with eyes that weren't brown, then they would be extremely unique.

Case 4: **If you could change your eye color to any color that you wanted, what color**
Hypothetical **would it be and why?**

If I could change my eye color to any color that I wanted, I would change it to green. Green is my favorite color and I think it would match with my hair color very well. Moreover, I heard that green is the color of intelligence so it would fit me even further.

Focus On: Accuracy / Response Technique

Technology

새로운 성형수술은 갈색 눈동자를 영구적으로 파란 눈동자로 바꾸는 데 까지 발전해왔다. 수술은 단 20초 정도 소요 되고 가격은 5,000달러 정도 소요 된다. 수술은 미국에서 장기 안전성 시험이 진행되는 동안에 이미 17명의 멕시코 환자와 20명의 코스타리카 환자가 주요 합병증 없이 시술이 진행되었다. 개발자는 정부의 안전성 허가가 처리되고 곧 일반 대중이 사용할 수 있을것으로 예상하고 있다.

Case 1: Opinion

이러한 성형수술에 대해 어떻게 생각합니까?

나는 그것이 멋진 기술 이라고 생각 하고 우리가 이러한 현대 기술을 우리에게 사용할 수 있는 것은 축복이라 생각합니다. 성형수술은 과거에 비해 오늘날은 좀 더 안전하고 가격도 많이 내려갔습니다. 이러한 이유때문에 한국에서 많은 사람들이 성형수술을 하게 되는 이유 중 하나라고 생각합니다.

Case 2: Personal

당신은 이러한 검증이 완료되지 않은 성형수술을 생각해 본적이 있습니까?

정상적인 상황에서는 어떠한 수술도 받고자 고려해 본적이 없습니다. 왜냐하면 제 건강을 위험속에 넣고 싶지 않기 때문입니다. 그러나 만약에 심각한 질병이 있고 수술로 고쳐질수 있다면 아마 고려해 볼 것 같습니다.

Case 3: General

눈동자 색깔을 바꾸면 어떠한 이점이 있을까요?

만약에 눈동자 색깔을 바꾸게 된다면, 당신은 좀 더 주목을 받을 것입니다. 특히 한국에서 더 통할 것 같습니다. 왜냐하면 모든 한국인들은 갈색 눈동자를 가지고 있으니까요. 만약에 갈색눈동자가 아닌 한국인이 있었다면 매우 독특했을 것입니다.

Case 4: Hypothetical

만약에 당신이 눈동자 색깔을 바꿀 수 있다면 어떤 색깔로 바꾸고 싶습니까? 이유는요?

만약에 내 눈동자 색깔을 바꿀 수 있다면 초록색으로 바꾸고 싶습니다. 초록색은 제가 가장 좋아하는 색깔이고 제 머리 색깔과 잘 어울릴 것 같습니다. 더 나아가 초록은 지혜의 색깔 이라고 들었기때문에 저한테 더욱 더 어울린다고 생각합니다.

Part 2: Listening Comprehension & Response Technique

Transportation

교통수단 지문은 듣기 문제에서 가장 흔하게 나오는 주제중의 하나이다.

Example passage:

Please listen carefully to the following paragraph about a new subway line and summarize it in your own words, giving as much information from the paragaph as possible. The paragraph can be repeated once.

The public transportation authority plans to expand the city's subway system. They will be adding a new express line that directly connects 10 of the city's busiest stations. Once complete, the new line is projected to become the most heavily used line in the city's subway system. While the majority of the public will benefit from this expansion, a small portion of the public will not. Roughly 15% of the public who don't ride the subway will still have to help pay for this new line.

Please summarize what you just heard in your own words, giving as much detail as possible.

Intro ....

Detail 1 ....

Detail 2 ....

Detail 3 ....

Inference ....

Transportation

Focus On: Accuracy / Response Technique

Possible follow up question to the listening passage:

Case 1: According to the paragraph, the city is planning to expand its subway system.
Opinion What is your opinion of your city's public transportation network?

....

....

Case 2: According to the paragraph, the city is planning to expand its subway system.
Personal What can your city do to improve its transportation network?

....

....

Case 3: According to the paragraph, the city is planning to expand its subway system.
General What are the advantages and disadvantages of having a subway system in a city?

....

....

Case 4: According to the paragraph, the city is planning to expand its subway system.
Hypothetical If your city wanted to use tax money to expand the public transportation in an area you never visit, would you still support it?

....

....

Part 2: Listening Comprehension & Response Technique

Transportation

The public transportation authority plans to expand the city's subway system. They will be adding a new express line that directly connects 10 of the city's busiest stations. Once complete, the new line is projected to become the most heavily used line in the city's subway system. While the majority of the public will benefit from this expansion, a small portion of the public will not. Roughly 15% of the public who don't ride the subway will still have to help pay for this new line.

Case 1: Opinion

What is your opinion of your city's public transportation network?

I think my city is doing a great job with the public transportation network, especially if you consider how large Seoul is. We have such a great public transportation network that many citizens don't even need a car to travel comfortably throughout the city.

Case 2: Personal

What can your city do to improve its transportation network?

I think my city needs to expand the amount of subway lines. Currently, there is only two major subway lines that runs north/south and both lines are incredibly crowded. We need a new north/south line so that there will be more city coverage and less people on the overcrowded lines.

Case 3: General

What are the advantages and disadvantages of having a subway system in a city?

The advantages of having a subway system is that it drastically reduces road traffic. Furthermore, it doesn't take up any land surface, which is great for crowded cities where land value is very high. The main disadvantage of subway systems is the cost and time to build them. Subway stations in my city typically take years to build. During that time, construction runs non-stop and is very noisy.

Case 4: Hypothetical

If your city wanted to use tax money to expand the public transportation in an area you never visit, would you still support it?

I think I would support it if I felt like the area that they were expanding was an important center such as a busy financial district or large shopping mall. If they decided to expand in an area that I didn't think needed a subway line such as low population zones, then I would not support the plans.

Focus On: Accuracy / Response Technique

Transportation

대중 교통 기관은 도시의 지하철 시스템을 연장하기로 계획하였다. 도시에서 가장 붐비는 10개의 역을 중간에 멈추지 않고 바로 연결하는 새로운 익스프레스 라인을 도입하는 것이다. 이것이 완성되면 새로운 노선은 도시 지하철 시스템에서 가장 많이 사용되는 노선이 될 것이다. 대부분의 대중이 수혜를 받는동안 소수의 대중들은 그렇지 않을 것이다. 대략 15%의 대중은 지하철은 이용하지 않지만 새로운 노선을 만드는데에 대한 세금 지불을 해야 한다.

Case 1: Opinion

당신이 살고 있는 도시의 대중교통 네트워크는 어떻습니까?

우리 도시는 대중교통 네트워크가 잘 되어 있다고 생각합니다. 특히 서울이 얼마나 큰지 생각해 보면 말입니다. 시민들이 차가 필요 없어도 될 만큼 서울 이곳 저곳을 편안하게 돌아다닐수 있는 훌륭한 대중교통 네트워크가 있습니다.

Case 2: Personal

당신의 도시에서 교통 네트워크를 향상시키기 위해서 무엇을 할 수 있습니까?

우리 도시는 지하철 라인 수를 확장해야 한다고 생각합니다. 현재 2개의 주요 지하철 라인이 북쪽과 남쪽으로 운영되고 있는데 믿을 수 없을 만큼 사람이 붐비고 있습니다. 새로운 북쪽/남쪽 라인을 추가해서 너무 붐비는 라인의 사람들을 분산 시킬 필요가 있습니다.

Case 3: General

도시에 지하철이 운행되는 것의 장단점은 무엇이라고 생각합니까?

지하철 시스템이 운행되는 것의 장점은 도로의 교통체증을 크게 줄여주는 것입니다. 또한 토지 표면을 차지하지 않기 때문에 토지 값이 비싸고 붐비는 곳에는 매우 좋다고 생각합니다. 지하철 시스템의 단점은 건설비용과 시간인것 같습니다. 우리 도시에서는 지하철역을 짓는데 몇 년이 걸리고 있습니다. 그 기간동안 건설이 계속 되어 매우 시끄럽습니다.

Case 4: Hypothetical

만약에 당신의 도시에서 당신이 전혀 가본적이 없는 지역에 대중교통을 연장하려고 세금을 사용한다면 이를 지지하겠습니까?

연장하려고 하는 지역이 붐비는 금융센터나 쇼핑몰 같은 중요한 곳이라면 지지할 것 같습니다. 그러나 적은 인구가 사는 곳에 지하철을 연장하려고 한다면 반대할 것 같습니다.

Part 2: Listening Comprehension & Response Technique

Current Affairs

최근 시사 지문은 다른 토픽들에 비해 자주 나오는 내용은 아니지만 1~2회 정도 시험 문제에 나온적이 있다. SPA에서의 최근 시사 토픽은 보통 정치나 종교 같은 논쟁거리가 될만한 주제는 피하고 있다.

Example passage:

Please listen carefully to the following paragraph about a new ordering machine and summarize it in your own words, giving as much information from the paragaph as possible. The paragraph can be repeated once.

McDonalds, the worldwide fast food giant, has recently installed 7,000 touch-screen ordering machines to serve some of its European customers. The machines, which come with a built in touch menu to take customer orders, are designed to replace some of the wage workers in their European restaurants. The move is projected to save the company millions of dollars in wages and also speed up service at their restaurants. However, the move comes at the cost of thousands of jobs lost to the automated machines.

Please summarize what you just heard in your own words, giving as much detail as possible.

Intro ....

Detail 1 ....

Detail 2 ....

Detail 3 ....

Inference ....

Focus On: Accuracy / Response Technique

Current Affairs

Possible follow up question to the listening passage:

Case 1:
Opinion

According to the paragraph, McDonalds installed new machines to take orders in place of human workers. What is your opinion of this?

....

....

Case 2:
Personal

According to the paragraph, McDonalds installed new machines to take orders in place of human workers. Have you ever ordered something electronically?

....

....

Case 3:
General

According to the paragraph, McDonalds installed new machines to take orders in place of human workers. What are some jobs that machines could never replace?

....

....

Case 4:
Hypothetical

According to the paragraph, McDonalds installed new machines to take orders in place of human workers. Do you think you could ever lose your job to a machine?

....

....

Current Affairs

McDonalds, the worldwide fast food giant, has recently installed 7,000 touch-screen ordering machines to serve some of its European customers. The machines, which come with a built in touch menu to take customer orders, are designed to replace some of the wage workers in their European restaurants. The move is projected to save the company millions of dollars in wages and also speed up service at their restaurants. However, the move comes at the cost of thousands of jobs lost to the automated machines.

Case 1: Opinion

According to the paragraph, McDonalds installed new machines to take orders in place of human workers. What is your opinion of this?

I think it's unfortunate that many people will lose jobs because of these new machines. However, at the same time, I feel that this is a technological step in the right direction. It will be interesting to see if McDonalds gets a lot of complaints about the new machines from their customers or if they will be happy about the switch.

Case 2: Personal

Have you ever ordered something electronically?

Yes, I have. I actually usually order McDonalds online. It's a lot easier than to go directly to the store to place an order. Their online site makes it easy for me to select whatever I want to eat from there menu. It only takes a minute for me to order online and they deliver the food straight to my home.

Case 3: General

According to the paragraph, McDonalds installed new machines to take orders in place of human workers. What are some jobs that machines could never replace?

I think there are certain high skill service jobs that machines could never replace such as doctors, lawyers, and chefs. In addition, machines will always need someone to take care of repairs and maintenance so people that maintain machines will probably never be replaced by machines.

Case 4: Hypothetical

According to the paragraph, McDonalds installed new machines to take orders in place of human workers. Do you think you could ever lose your job to a machine?

I don't think I will ever lose my job in my lifetime. However, the way machine technology is evolving, I think it might be possible in about a hundred years. Hopefully, by the time this technology is around, I will be retired already.

Focus On: Accuracy / Response Technique

Current Affairs

글로벌 패스트푸드 체인인 맥도날드가 최근에 7,000대의 터치스크린 주문 기계를 설치해서 유럽 고객에게 서비스를 제공하고 있다. 고객 주문을 받기 위해 내장된 터치 메뉴 기계는 유럽 레스토랑에서 임금 노동자를 대신하기 위해 디자인 되었다. 이러한 움직임은 수백만 달러의 임금을 절약하고 레스토랑의 서비스 속도를 높일 것으로 예상했다. 그러나 이러한 움직임은 자동화 기계로 인해 수천의 일자리가 줄어들었다.

Case 1: Opinion

문장에 따르면, 맥도날드가 인간을 대신해서 주문을 받는 새로운 주문 기계를 설치했다고 합니다. 이것에 대해 어떻게 생각합니까?

새로운 기계 때문에 많은 사람들이 일자리를 잃게되는 불행한 일이라고 생각합니다. 그러나 동시에 인류를 위한 기술 발전 단계의 옳은 방향이라고도 생각됩니다. 맥도날드가 새로운 기계로 고객들에게 많은 불평을 받을지 아니면 고객들이 더 만족해할지 흥미로운 일이 될 것입니다.

Case 2: Personal

기계로 무엇인가 주문을 해 본 적이 있습니까?

네, 있습니다. 보통 맥도날드 햄버거를 주문할때 온라인으로 주문합니다. 매장에가서 직접 주문하는 것보다 훨씬 간편합니다. 맥도날드 홈페이지에 들어가면 원하는 것을 주문할 수 있도록 잘 구비되어 있습니다. 단 몇분안에 온라인에서 주문하면 집으로 배달까지 해줍니다.

Case 3: General

문장에 따르면, 맥도날드가 인간을 대신해서 주문을 받는 새로운 주문 기계를 설치했다고 합니다. 어떠한 직업이 기계가 절대 대체할 수 없다고 생각합니까?

의사나 변호사, 요리사 같이 특별한 기술이 필요한 직업에서는 대체가 어려울것이라고 생각합니다. 게다가 기계는 항상 누군가가 고치고 유지보수를 해야하는데 이러한 유지보수를 하는 사람들 역시 기계가 대체할 수 없는 직업이라고 생각합니다.

Case 4: Hypothetical

문장에 따르면, 맥도날드가 인간을 대신해서 주문을 받는 새로운 주문 기계를 설치했다고 합니다. 당신은 기계가 당신의 직업을 빼앗아 일자리를 잃을 것이라고 생각합니까?

제 생전에는 직업을 잃을 것 같지 않습니다. 그러나 기계 기술이 발전해서 100년후에는 제 직업이 빼앗길 수도 있을 것 같습니다. 바라건데 이러한 기술의 발전이 제가 은퇴한 이후에 이루어 졌으면 합니다.

SPA In-Depth Part 3

Content & Use of Vocabulary
Focus on: Content / Vocab

Question Categories:
- Finance
- Travel
- Work
- Education
- Relationship
- Technology
- Trends
- Health

Part 3: Content & Use of Vocabulary

Preview

Q3 Many people prefer taking the bus over taking the subway. Why do you think this is?

....

Follow up Which mode of transportation do you prefer more?

....

Overview

- Part 3의 배점은 12점이다.
- Part 3에서는 세부적인 내용의 답변과 답변의 근거를 정확히 이야기 해주어야 점수 배점이 높다.
- 단어의 선택과 사용 역시 점수 배점에서 중요한 부분이기 때문에 Part 3에서는 자신이 알고 있는 단어의 실력 발휘가 필요하다.

Tip

- 길게 답변을 하기 보다는 적절한 속담이나 패턴을 활용하여 어휘 능력을 보여주는 핵심

- 단어 선택에 있어 평소에 알고 있던 기본적인 단어보다는 고급 단어를 사용할 것.

- 같은 단어의 반복을 피할 것.

  Academic, Business Language에서는 다양한 어휘를 활용

Example Happy = glad = pleased = delighted

Focus On: Content / Vocabulary

Sample

Part 3 Question — Many people prefer taking the bus over the subway. Why do you think this is?

Response — I think many people prefer taking the bus over the subway because there are a lot more bus routes and bus stops compared to subway stations. If you take the bus, you can get on and get off at locations that are much more convenient.

Follow up — Which mode of transportation do you prefer more?

Response — I actually prefer taking the subway because during rush hour, the subway is a lot faster. In addition, the subway is a lot smoother. I hate all the bumps and turns you have to endure while riding on a bus.

Part 3: Content & Use of Vocabulary

Strategy

- Part 3는 답변한 내용에 대한 "Quality"에 대해 채점이 이루어진다.

- 답변을 할때 답변에 대한 근거를 충분히 갖고 대답을 하게 되면 좋은 점수를 받을 수 있다.

- Part 3에서는 Part 1과는 달리 "발음"이나 "페이스"에 대해 따로 채점을 하지 않으므로 여기서는 발음 보다는 충분한 근거 제시의 어휘 사용 능력을 보여주면 된다.

- 만약에 답변하기에 생각할 시간이 필요하면 평가위원에게 편안하게 질문을 하며 생각할 시간을 가져보는 것도 좋다. (pg 229 filler phrases 참고)

- 또한 part 1과는 다르게 part 3에서는 답변의 길이도 중요하며 대답의 핵심도 중요하다 (Main Point, Supporting details). 평가위원은 당신의 문법이나 발음보다는 아이디어와 단어 사용에 더 초점을 두고 채점을 하게 된다.

- 단어는 평소에 익숙한 단어와 함께 고급 단어들도 부담갖지 말고 실전에서 사용되어져야 하고 이때 1~2개의 Key Vocabulary 단어가 Part 3에서 점수를 확실히 올려줄 것이다

Part 3 Q Structure

<u>Many people prefer taking the bus over taking the subway.</u> Why do you think this is?
                    Topic Sentence

- Part 3의 질문은 항상 Topic Sentence 에 대한 몇 가지 정보를 제공하는 주제 문장 으로 시작한다.

- 그 다음에 토픽에 대한 의견을 물어보는 질문이 이어진다. (Follow Up)

- SPA 질문에서는 일반적으로 정치나 종교같이 논란이 큰 질문에 대해서는 피하고 있으므로 이러한 주제에 대해서는 따로 준비하지 않아도 좋다

- Follow up 문제는 토픽에 대한 당신 의견에 입각해서 질문이 던져지게 되는데 보통 당신의 답변 깊에에 따라 결정 지어 지게 된다.

- 만약에 평가위원이 토픽에 대해 당신의 의견을 더 듣고 싶으면 토픽에 관련된 개인적인 질문이 이루어 질 것이다.

Focus On: Content / Vocabulary

Note

Response   I think <u>many people prefer taking the bus over the subway</u>
                                                                     Topic
because <u>there are a lot more bus routes and bus stops compared
to subway stations.</u>   If you take the bus, <u>you can get on and get
off at locations that are much more convenient.</u>

- 위의 대답에서 화자는 Topic의 대답과 Reason으로 끝나지 않고 Supporting detail을 이용하여 Reason을 더욱 명확하게 설명해 주었다.

- 위의 대답에는 화자의 개인 의견을 설명하지 않았기 때문에 아마도 SPA평가위원은 아래와 같이 개인적인 질문을 추가적이 이루어 질 수 있다.

Follow Up   Which mode of transportation do you prefer more?

Response   <u>I actually prefer taking the subway</u> because <u>during **rush hour**, the
subway is a lot faster.</u> In addition, <u>the subway is a lot **smoother**.</u> <u>I
hate all the bumps and turns you have to **endure** while riding on
a bus.</u>

Pro Tip

1. Part 3는 대답에 있어서 얼마나 정확한 단어를 사용하느냐가 중요하다..
위의 Response에서 **rush hour** 단어 사용이 추가 점수로 이루어 질 것이다.

2. **Smoother** 단어역시 추가 점수가 된다. 묘사를 위한 단어를 사용 했기 때문이다.

3. **Endure** 단어가 추가 점수로 이루어 진다. 이 단어는 보통 Non-Native 자주 사용하는 단어가 아니기 때문이다.

Part 3: Content & Use of Vocabulary

Finance

Topic Sentence: More and more people are using credit cards to pay for expensive purchases.

Case 1: What are the advantages and disadvantages of using a credit card for expensive purchases?

....

....

Case 2: What are your thoughts on this trend?

....

....

Case 3: Do you think it's a good idea to make expensive purchases with a credit card.

....

....

Case 4: Do you use credit cards on expensive purchases?

....

....

Case 5: Do you prefer using a credit card or cash for purchases?

....

....

Focus On: Content / Vocabulary

Travel

Topic Sentence: With China's expanding middle class, more and more Chinese tourists are traveling abroad.

Case 1: What are the advantages and disadvantages of having more Chinese tourists visit Korea?

....

....

Case 2: What are your thoughts on this trend?

....

....

Case 3: What are the effects of there being more Chinese tourists worldwide?

....

....

Case 4: Why do you think Chinese tourists would want to visit Korea?

....

....

Case 5: Do you prefer having more or less tourists visit Korea?

....

....

Part 3 Practice

Part 3: Content & Use of Vocabulary

Work

Topic Sentence   Among OECD countries, Koreans work the most hours while having one of the lowest overall productivity outputs per worker.

Case 1   Why do you think this is?

....

....

Case 2   What are your thoughts on this statement?

....

....

Case 3   What is your opinion of this?

....

....

Case 4   Do you think Koreans should work less hours?

....

....

Case 5   How do you think Koreans can increase productivity?

....

....

Focus On: Content / Vocabulary

Education

Topic Sentence Some schools are increasing the amount of physical education while other schools are decreasing the amount.

Case 1 What are the advantages and disadvantages of having physical education classes in schools?

....

....

Case 2 What are your thoughts on this?

....

....

Case 3 Do you think having more physical education time in schools is a good thing or a bad thing?

....

....

Case 4 Why do you think physical education class is important for children's education?

....

....

Case 5 Do you think it is better to have more physical education time or less?

....

....

Part 3: Content & Use of Vocabulary

Relationship

Topic Sentence — Some people say that having arguments in a relationship is a good thing.

Case 1 — Why do you think this is?

....

....

Case 2 — What are your thoughts on this statement?

....

....

Case 3 — What is your opinion of this?

....

....

Case 4 — Do you think having arguments can positively impact a relationship?

....

....

Case 5 — How do you feel after arguing with someone you are close with?

....

....

Technology

Topic Sentence   Some people believe that robots will eventually take over most of our current jobs.

Case 1   What are the advantages and disadvantages of robots taking over our jobs?

....

....

Case 2   What are your thoughts on this?

....

....

Case 3   Do you think robots will eventually take over all jobs?

....

....

Case 4   Are there any jobs that robots could never take over?

....

....

Case 5   Do you think robots taking over jobs is a good thing or a bad thing?

....

....

Part 3: Content & Use of Vocabulary

Trends

Topic Sentence The birth rate has been on the decline in Korea.

Case 1 Why do you think this is?

....

....

Case 2 What are your thoughts on this trend?

....

....

Case 3 What is your opinion of this?

....

....

Case 4 What are the potential consequences if this trend continues?

....

....

Case 5 How do think the government should address this issue?

....

....

Focus On: Content / Vocabulary

Health

Topic Sentence — Health is something that most people value highly in their lives.

Case 1 — How do you take care of your health?

....

....

Case 2 — Do you live a healthy life?

....

....

Case 3 — Why is your health important to you?

....

....

Case 4 — Would you rather work out or diet?

....

....

Case 5 — Do you think you are fit?

....

....

Part 3 Practice

Finance

More and more people are using credit cards to pay for expensive purchases.

Case 1 — What are the advantages and disadvantages of using a credit card for expensive purchases?

One of the advantages of using a credit card for expensive purchases is that you can spread the payment out rather than paying all at once. Another advantage is that many credit cards offer special bonuses like cash back. A disadvantage is that there is interest if your balance is not fully paid off. In addition, if you're late on a payment, there are a lot of fees that get added on.

Case 2 — What are your thoughts on this trend?

I think that this is a good trend. Credit cards make spending a lot more convenient. Rather than carrying a wallet full of cash, I can just carry one card and not have to worry about running out of money.

Case 3 — Do you think it's a good idea to make expensive purchases with a credit card.

Yes, I think it's a good idea because it leaves a record of my purchase. If I pay with cash, the only record is a receipt which is easy to lose. If I ever need to return a product or exchange it, having the credit card record helps make exchanging the product easier.

Case 4 — Do you use credit cards on expensive purchases?

No, I don't use credit cards for expensive purchases. The reason why I don't use credit cards is because I worry about spending too much money. When I use a credit card, my spending sometimes goes out of control.

Case 5 — Do you prefer using a credit card or cash for purchases?

I prefer using a credit card because it's a lot more convenient. I'd rather have one credit card than a fat wallet full of cash.

Focus On: Content / Vocabulary

Finance

비싼 물건 구입시에 신용카드를 사용하는 사람들이 늘어나고 있다.

Case 1   신용카드로 비싼 물건을 구입하는 것의 장단점은 무엇입니까?

비싼 물건을 구입시에 신용카드 사용의 장점은 할부 지불이 가능하다는 것이다. 또 다른 장점은 많은 카드 회사들이 캐쉬백 같은 보너스를 제공하는 것에 있다. 단점은 할부 지불에 수수료가 있으며 지불일을 지키지 않으면 역시 많은 이자가 붙는다는 점이다.

Case 2   이러한 트렌드에 대해서 어떻게 생각하는가? (비싼 물건을 신용카드로 구매하는 것)

내 생각에는 좋은 트렌드인 것 같다. 신용카드는 많은 편리함을 가져오게 만들었다. 지갑에 돈을 가득 채워 갖고 다니는 것보다 신용카드 한장 갖고 다니면 돈 잃어버릴 거적을 하지 않아도 된다.

Case 3   신용카드로 비싼 물건을 사는 것이 좋은 생각이라고 생각합니까?

네, 좋은 생각이라고 생각합니다. 왜냐하면 구입후에 기록이 남으니까요. 만약에 현금으로 계산을 하게 되면 영수증에만 기록이 남고 또 잃어버리기도 쉬워요. 만약에 제품을 반품을 하거나 교환이 필요할때 신용카드 기록이 제품을 교환할때 도움을 줄 수 있습니다.

Case 4   당신은 비싼 물건을 구입할때 신용카드를 사용합니까?

아니요, 저는 비싼 물건을 구입할때 신용카드를 사용하지 않습니다. 신용카드를 사용하지 않는 이유는 너무 많은 돈을 쓸까봐 걱정되기 때문입니다. 신용카드를 사용하게 되면 조절없이 남용하여 사용되기 때문입니다.

Case 5   물건을 구입할때 신용카드와 현금중 어느쪽을 사용하십니까?

저는 신용카드 사용을 선호합니다. 왜냐하면 더 편리하니까요. 지갑에 현급을 가득 채워 다니는 것보다 신용카드 한장 넣는 것이 더 좋아요.

Travel

With China's expanding middle class, more and more Chinese tourists are traveling abroad.

Case 1 — **What are the advantages and disadvantages of having more Chinese tourists visit Korea?**

The biggest advantage of there being more Chinese tourists in Korea is that local businesses can profit from the increased number of customers, especially in places like Myeongdong where there are many shops for tourists to shop at. A possible disadvantage might be that a few Chinese tourists may not know or follow local etiquette.

Case 2 — **What are your thoughts on this trend?**

Overall, I think it's great. More Chinese visitors means more customers for businesses. It's also good for China because I think the more global their citizens become, the more China will try to cooperate with other countries.

Case 3 — **What are the effects of there being more Chinese tourists worldwide?**

I think countries that embrace Chinese tourists will benefit a lot from the increased amount of tourists. China's quickly becoming one of the most important economies in the world so having their citizens spend their money worldwide helps the global market.

Case 4 — **Why do you think Chinese tourists would want to visit Korea?**

I think Chinese tourists would want to visit Korea because Korean dramas as well as Korean music is very popular in China. Also, the countries are close geographically so it's not too expensive to travel here.

Case 5 — **Do you prefer having more or less tourists visit Korea?**

I prefer having more tourists visit Korea. We need tourists to help expand our economy. If we didn't have any tourists, many businesses here would fail.

Focus On: Content / Vocabulary

Travel

중산층의 중국인이 늘어날수록 해외 여행하는 중국 여행객 수가 늘어나고 있다.

Case 1   **한국 방문하는 중국 관광객이 증가하는 것에 대한 장단점은 무엇입니까?**

한국에 중국 관광객이 늘어나면 가장 큰 장점은 관광객의 숫자에 따라 한국 내수시장이 클수 있다는 점이다. 특히 명동같이 많은 관광객이 모여 드는 곳은 많은 이익을 볼 수 있을 것이다. 일어날 수 있는 단점으로는 몇 몇의 중국인들은 한국 현지 에티켓을 지키지 않을 수 있다는 점이다.

Case 2   **이러한 트렌드에 대해서 어떻게 생각하는가? (중국 관광객이 늘어나는것)**

종합적으로 이것은 좋은 현상이라고 생각합니다. 중국 관광객이 늘어난다는 뜻은 비즈니스 고객이 늘어난다는 뜻입니다. 또한 중국에게도 좋은 현상입니다. 좀더 시민들이 국제화 될 수 있는 기회이기도 하며 중국이 다른 나라들과 함께 협력 관계를 맺는 것을 노력할 거라 생각합니다.

Case 3   **세계적으로 중국 관광객이 늘어나면 생겨나는 영향이 무엇이라 생각합니까?**

제 생각에는 중국 관광객을 받아 들이는 국가들은 관광객 수가 늘어나는 것으로부터 막대한 이익을 거둘 수 있을 거라 생각됩니다. 중국은 빠르게 세계에서 가장 중요한 경제국가가 되가고 있고 시민들에게 해외에서 돈을 쓰게 함으로서 국제 시장에서도 도움이 될 것이다.

Case 4   **중국 관광객이 왜 한국에 오고 싶어하는 것일까요?**

한국 드라마와 음악이 중국에서 인기가 많기 때문에 한국에 오고 싶어 하는 것 같습니다. 또한 지리적으로 가깝기 때문에 한국으로 오는 것은 비싸지 않으니까요.

Case 5   **한국에 관광객이 늘어나는것과 줄어드는것 어느 쪽이 더 좋습니까?**

저는 한국에 관광객이 늘어나는것이 더 좋습니다. 관광객이 늘어나서 경제가 좋아져야 합니다. 관광객이 줄어들면 많은 비즈니스 산업이 망할수도 있습니다.

Work

Among OECD countries, Koreans work the most hours while having one of the lowest overall productivity outputs per worker.

Case 1
Why do you think this is?

I think perhaps it's because bosses in Korea often look more at how many hours an employee works rather than the fruit of their productivity. People often slack off at work because they know bosses only look at the start and finish times of employees when giving performance evaluations.

Case 2
What are your thoughts on this trend?

I think this statement is somewhat accurate. Most of the people I work with work very long hours but get very little done. I think a lot of it has to do with overtime wages. Many workers want to make more money so will try to stretch out their work for as long as possible.

Case 3
What is your opinion of this?

I think it's unfair in a way because per hour, we are also paid one of the lowest wages among OECD countries. I think if wages improve, productivity will also improve due to the increased motivation to keep your job.

Case 4
Do you think Koreans should work less hours?

I think it depends. Some people want to make more money so will try to work more hours. I, on the other hand, want to just start at 9 am and leave by 6 pm. Overall, I think there are more people that want to work less hours than work more hours.

Case 5
How do you think Koreans can increase productivity?

Most Koreans stay late not because they are busy but because they don't want to look bad by leaving earlier than other workers. If Koreans stop looking at how long people stay at work as a measure of productivity, then I think Koreans can increase productvity per working hour.

Focus On: Content / Vocabulary

Work

OECD 국가중 한국은 가장 많은 시간 일을하면서 근로자당 생산력이 가장 낮은 국가이다.

Case 1 가장 많은 근로시간에 생산력이 떨어지는 이유는 무엇 때문인것 같습니까?

제 생각에는 아마도 한국에서는 직장상사가 직원을 평가할때 결과물보다는 얼마나 오랫동안 일을 했는지를 보기 때문인 것 같습니다. 이때문에 사람들은 좀더 빈둥대면서 일을 하게 될 것입니다. 왜냐하면 상사가 직원들이 얼마나 오랜시간 남아있는지만 보고 업무 평가를 하기 때문입니다.

Case 2 이런 상황에 대해 당신은 어떻게 생각합니까?

저는 이 상황이 어느정도 정확하다고 생각합니다. 제가 일하는 곳의 대부분의 사람들은 긴시간 일을 하지만 일의 완성도는 매우 적습니다. 아마 이렇게 일을 하는 이유는 근무외 수당 때문인 것 같습니다. 많은 근로자들이 좀 더 많은 돈을 벌기를 희망하기 때문에 가능한 한 오랫동안 자기 자리에 앉아 일을 하는 것 같습니다.

Case 3 이런 상황에 대한 당신의 의견은 어떻습니까?

어떤 면에서 이것은 불공평합니다. 왜냐하면 한국의 시간당 임금은 OECD국가증에 가장 낮은 국가중의 하나이기 때문입니다. 만약에 임금을 올리게 된다면 업무에 대한 동기부여로 인해 생산력도 올라가게 될 거라 생각합니다.

Case 4 당신이 생각하기에 한국인은 근무시간이 줄어들어야 한다고 생각합니까?

상황에 따라 다르다고 생각합니다. 어떤 사람들은 돈을 더 많이 벌고 싶어서 더 많은 시간 일을 할 수도 있습니다. 저 같은 경우 그냥 아침 9시부터 저녁 6시까지만 일하고 싶습니다. 전체적으로는 근무시간을 줄이고 싶어하는 사람이 더 많을 것 같습니다.

Case 5 어떻게 한국인이 생산력을 높일수 있다고 생각합니까?

대부분의 한국 사람들은 바빠서가 아니라 다른 직원들보다 일찍 가는 것에 대한 눈치 때무에 늦게 있게 되다 마약에 한국사람들의 의식이 야근을 해야 생산력이 높다는 것을 고치게 된다면 실제 시간당 생산력은 높아질 것이라 생각합니다.

Part 3 Practice

Education

Some schools are increasing the amount of physical education while other schools are decreasing the amount.

Case 1 — What are the advantages and disadvantages of having physical education classes in schools?

The biggest advantage is that students are a lot healthier with physical education classes. Being healthy helps studnets concentrate better in class and will therefore also help with their studies. A disadvantage is that it takes away valuable class time that could be used to teach other essential subjects like math and science.

Case 2 — What are your thoughts on this statement?

I think it's better to increase the amount of time students spend in physical education class. Children these days are a lot more obese than they were in the past. To combat the increasing childhood obesity problem, we need to increase physical education time.

Case 3 — Do you think having more physical education time in schools is a good thing or a bad thing?

I think it's a bad thing. Students should be studying in school, not running around and playing. There are plenty of opportunities to exercise outside of school so I don't think having exercise in school is absolutely necessary.

Case 4 — Why do you think some schools are decreasing the amount of physical education classes?

I believe that some schools are decreasing the amount of physical education classes because it's not considered to be an essential part of the curriculum. Compared to classes like math, science, and history, people don't view physical education class as important.

Case 5 — Do you think it is better to have more physical education time or less?

I think it's better to have less physical education time. The reason I think that however, is not because I don't think physical education is important. It's because I think students already spend too much time at school. I think they should have shorter classes in general, not just physical education.

Education

대부분의 학교들이 체육 수업을 줄이는 동안 어떤 학교들은 체육수업 시간을 늘리고 있습니다.

Case 1   **학교에서의 체육수업을 갖는것에 대한 장단점은 무엇입니까?**

체육수업의 가장 큰 장점은 학생들이 더욱 건강해 질 것이라는 것이다. 건강해지는 것은 학교 공부에 더 집중할 수 있게 해주고 결국은 공부에도 도움이된다. 단점은 수학이나 영어같은 필수적인 수업을 할 수 있는 시간이 줄어 든다는 것이다.

Case 2   **이러한 의견에 어떻게 생각하십니까?**

제 생각에는 체육수업 시간을 늘리는것이 더 났다고 생각합니다.
요즘 어린이들은 과거보다 더 비만이 늘었습니다. 증가하고 있는 아동 비만문제를 위해 체육수업시간이 더 늘어나야 한다고 생각합니다.

Case 3   **학교에서 체육수업 시간이 늘어나는것이 좋은 현상입니까? 나쁜 현상입니까?**

저는 나쁜현상이라고 봅니다. 학생들은 학교에서 공부를 해야합니다. 뛰고 놀고 그러면 안됩니다. 방과후에 밖에서 뛰어 놀며 운동할 수 있는 기회가 많습니다. 그렇기 때문에 저는 체육수업이 꼭 필요한 수업이라고 생각하지 않습니다.

Case 4   **어떤 학교는 왜 체육수업을 줄이고 있는 것일까요?**

어떤 학교들은 체육수업을 줄이고 있는데 그 이유는 필수 교육과정을 고려하지 않았기 때문입니다. 수학, 과학 역사같은 과목과 비교해서 체육수업은 동등하게 중요하다고 여기지 않기 때문이다.

Case 5   **체육수업을 늘리는 것이 좋을까요? 줄이는 것이 좋을까요?**

제 생각에는 체육수업을 줄이는게 좋다고 생각합니다. 그렇게 생각하는 것은 체육수업이 중요하지 않다기 이니리 학생들은 이미 학교에서 니무 많은 시긴을 보내고 있기 때문입니다. 단순히 체육수업뿐 아니라 전체적으로 수업이 줄어들어야 한다고 생각합니다.

Relationship

Some people say that having arguments in a relationship is a good thing.

Case 1
Why do you think this is?

I think it's because arguments are usually the first step towards understanding each other better. If you never argue, that usually means at least one person is holding something back. It's probably better to be honest with each other even if it means a little bit of arguing.

Case 2
What are your thoughts on this statement?

I know that every relationship is bound to have some arguments but I don't think it's necessarily a good thing. People usually argue because they disagree on something. I would rather be in a relationship with someone who generally has the same values as I do.

Case 3
What is your opinion of this?

I agree with this statement to a certain extend. I think arguments can make things more interesting if done in moderate amounts. I argue with my wife from time to time but I think that's a healthy part of our relationship because it allows us to express how we truly feel.

Case 4
Do you think having arguments can positively impact a relationship?

Yes, I think it can as long as you can resolve them. Arguments often lead to a better understanding of a person's true feelings. If your relationship can survive an argument, it usually means that you can tolerate or even appreciate the other person's true feelings.

Case 5
How do you feel after arguing with someone you are close with?

It would depend on what we argued about but I usually feel either angry or sad after an argument with someone I'm close with. If I get angry, I usually feel motivated to do something so that can sometimes be a good thing. However, if I feel sad, I will probably apologize to whoever I argued with.

Focus On: Content / Vocabulary

Relationship

어떤 사람들은 말다툼 하는것이 관계 개선에 좋은 것이라고 이야기 합니다.

Case 1 왜 그렇다고 생각합니까?

말 다툼은 서로를 더 잘 이해하는데 한 발짝 다가가는 것이라고 생각합니다.
만약에 한번도 말 다툼을 하지 않으면 적어도 한사람은 뒤에 무엇인가 감추고 있다는 뜻입니다. 서로에게 정직한것이 더 좋다고 생각합니다. 이것이 말다툼으로 이루어지더라도.

Case 2 이러한 의견에 어떻게 생각합니까?

어떤 관계이든 말 다툼할 가능성이 있습니다. 그러나 반드시 좋은것이라 생각하지 않습니다. 사람들이 말 다툼할때는 보통 서로 무엇인가에 동의하지 않기 때문에 일어납니다. 저는 오히려 저와 같은 가치를 가지고 있는 사람과 관계를 맺고 싶습니다.

Case 3 이러한 이야기에 당신 의견은 어떻습니까?

이 이야기에 어느정도 동의합니다. 어느정도의 말 싸움은 삶을 즐겁게 한다고 생각합니다. 저는 아내와 매 시간 싸우는데 우리 관계에 있어서 건강한 상태라고 생각합니다. 왜냐하면 자신이 어떻게 생각하는지 진실되게 표현을 하게 되니깐요.

Case 4 말 다툼이 관계에 있어서 긍정적인 영향을 준다고 생각합니까?

네, 당신이 풀어나갈수 있는 동안은 말 다툼이 서로의 진심을 더 잘 이해할수 있도록 이끌어 줍니다. 만약에 당신의 관계가 말 다툼후 잘 해결이 되었다면 상대방의 진심을 받아들일수 있거나 감사할 수 있다는 뜻입니다.

Case 5 가까운 사람과 말 다툼을 한 후에 기분이 어떠합니까?

어떤 주제로 인해 말 다툼 했냐에 따라 다르지만 보통 가까운 사람과 말 다툼을 하게되면 화가 나거나 슬픔니다. 만약에 화나게 되면 무엇인가를 하는데 있어서 동기부여가 되어 기끔 좋은 계기가 되기도 하지만 만약에 슬프게 되면 말 다툼을 잊고 상대방에게 사과를 할 것입니다.

Technology

Some people believe that robots will eventually take over most of our current jobs.

Case 1 **What are the advantages and disadvantages of robots taking over our jobs?**

The advantages of robots taking over our jobs is that things will become cheaper because there won't be a cost for labor. In addition, if the job happens to be a dangerous job like coal mining or space exploration, then there won't be any human lives at risk. The biggest disadvantage is that there will be less jobs for people so finding a job will become more challenging.

Case 2 **What are your thoughts on this?**

I think it's a little scary and we should make sure we are always in control of our robots. In a recent interview, I heard that Stephen Hawking made a warning about robots eventually taking over the world. Normally, I would think this sort of scenario as science fiction but because one of the world's smartest people said it, it leaves me worried.

Case 3 **Do you think robots will eventually take over all jobs?**

I can see that as a possibility. Many menial jobs are already being automated and robotics seems to be evolving exponentially. I think for a while, there will be a need for skilled human workers to build and maintain the robots. However, I think even those jobs will eventually be replaced by robots.

Case 4 **Are there any jobs that robots could never take over?**

I think robots could never take over jobs that require human talent such as sports or acting. Another thing robots could never take over is raising children. I don't think robots will ever replace mothers.

Case 5 **Do you think robots taking over jobs is a good thing or a bad thing?**

I think it's a double edged sword. On one hand, its a sign that human technology will eventually free us from having to work at all. However, the bad thing is that presently, people need jobs to make a living. Until the point comes where robots can do all jobs and make any service free, people will need jobs to pay for services.

Focus On: Content / Vocabulary
Technology

어떤 사람들은 결국 로봇이 현재 우리의 일자리를 모두 빼앗을 것이라고 믿습니다.

Case 1 **로봇이 일자리를 대체하는 것에 대한 장단점은 무엇입니까?**

로봇이 우리의 일자리를 대신하는 거에 대한 장점은 물가가 낮아 질수 있다는 것입니다. 인력에 대한 임금이 들어가지 않기 때문입니다. 게다가 광산이나 우주 비행사같이 위험한 직업에 투입이 된다면 사람들은 위험에 처해서 살지 않아도 됩니다. 가장 큰 단점은 일자리가 줄어들어 사람들이 직업을 찾기 더욱 더 힘들어질 것이라는 것입니다.

Case 2 **이러한 의견에 당신은 어떻게 생각합니까?**

조금 무섭기도하고 우리가 로봇을 완벽히 통제할 수 있다는 것에 대한 확신이 필요합니다. Stephen Hawking의 최근 인터뷰에서 결국 로봇이 세계를 지배할 것이라고 경고하였습니다. 일반적으로 이런 시나리오는 공상과학 이야기라 생각하지만 세계의 석학들이 이러한 이야기를 하게되면 걱정이 됩니다.

Case 3 **로봇이 결국에는 모든 일자리를 대체할 거라고 생각합니까?**

저는 가능하다고 봅니다. 많은 3D일자리들이 이미 자동화되었고 로봇들이 기하급수적으로 진화가 될거라 생각됩니다. 얼마동안은 적어도 숙련공들이 남아서 로봇을 만들고 유지보수할거라 생각하지만 결국에는 이러한 숙련공들의 자리도 로봇공학의 발전으로 대체가 될것이라 생각합니다.

Case 4 **로봇이 절대 대체할수 없는 일자리가 있을 것 같습니까?**

인간의 재능이 필요한 스포츠나 연기 분야의 직업은 대체될 수 없을 것 같습니다. 또 다른 대체불가능한 분야는 아이를 키우고 교육시키는 것입니다. 로봇은 어머니를 대신하는 역할은 못힐 것 같습니다.

Case 5 **로봇이 일자리를 대체하는 것이 좋다고 봅니까? 나쁘다고 봅니까?**

제 생각에 이것은 양날의 검 문제입니다. 어떤 면에서는 마침내 인간의 기술이 우리를 노동에서 해방 시켜주는 신호이기도 합니다. 그러니 이 시점까지는 사람들이 살기 위해 일자리가 필요하기 때문에 좋다고 볼 수 없습니다. 로봇이 모든 일자리를 대체하고 어떠한 서비스든 무료로 해주는 시점이 올때까지는 사람들은 서비스 지불을 위해 일자리가 필요할 것입니다..

Trends

The birth rate has been on the decline in Korea.

Case 1
Why do you think this is?

I think the main reason for the decline in birth rate is because of the increasing cost of living. It's becoming more and more expensive to raise a family. For this reason, many young people, who are having enough difficulty just making a living, are prioritizing financial stability over raising a family.

Case 2
What are your thoughts on this trend?

I think this trend reflects the rapid modernization of Korea's society. In the past, Korean families needed many children to help with farming and running family businesses. These days, children are a financial liability rather than an asset.

Case 3
What is your opinion of this?

I think it's a good thing because our country already feels overpopulated. I think it would be great for the world in fact if every country had a declining birth rate. Overpopulation is already a huge problem globally so I think this is a step in the right direction for mankind.

Case 4
What are the potential consequences if this trend continues?

I think it's a sign of bad things to come. Our workforce is aging but we won't have enough young people to replace them once they retire. With not enough workers and a large senior population to support, I think the few young people that are working will have difficulty supporting our country.

Case 5
How do you think the government can address this issue?

I think the government can offer young couples more incentives to have children. One of the biggest hurdles for not having children is finding affordable housing in a child friendly neighborhood. If the government offers some sort of aid with this, I think more couples will have children.

Trends

한국에서 출생율이 떨어지고 있습니다.

Case 1   **한국의 출산율이 왜 떨어진다고 생각합니까?**

출산율이 떨어지는 이유는 생활비가 올라가고 있기 때문인것 같습니다.
가족 부양하기에 갈수록 비싸지고 있기 때문에 이미 사는데 충분히 어려움을 겪는
젊은이들은 가족부양보다는 금전적인 안정성을 우선시 하고 있습니다.

Case 2   **이러한 현상에 대해 어떻게 생각하십니까?**

저는 이러한 추세가 한국사회의 급속한 현대화를 반영하고 있다고 생각합니다.
과거 한국인의 가정은 많은 자식들이 농사와 가족 비즈니스를 도와주어야 했습니다. 그러나
오늘날에는 자식들은 가족의 자산이라기 보다는 돈이 들어가는 대상이 되었습니다.

Case 3   **출산율이 떨어지는 추세에 대해 어떤 의견이 있습니까?**

제 생각에는 좋은 추세라고 생각합니다. 왜냐하면 우리나라는 이미 인구가 너무 많기
때문입니다. 세계적으로도 각 나라가 출산율이 떨어지는게 좋다고 본다. 과도한
인구밀도는 이미 세계적으로 커다란 문제이기 때문에 인류를 위해 좋은 방향으로 가는
발걸음이라고 봅니다.

Case 4   **이러한 현상이 지속되면 잠재적인 위험은 무엇이 있을 것 같습니까?**

나쁜 영향이 올거라는 신호인거 같습니다. 우리의 노동력은 고령화가 되가고 있으나 그들이
은퇴하고 나서 대체할 젊은 사람들은 부족할 것입니다. 충분치 않은 노동자들이 많은
고령인구들을 먹여살려야 합니다. 이때문에 우리나라를 지탱하는데 소수의 젊은이들이
어려움을 겪을 것입니다.

Case 5   **정부가 이러한 이슈에 대해 어떻게 해결할 수 있다고 생각합니까?**

정부가 젊은 신혼부부에게 아이를 갖는거에 대해서 인센티브를 주어야 한다고 생각합니다.
아이를 갖지 않는 가장 큰 걸림돌은 아기를 키우기 위한 좋은 지역의 저렴한 집을 찾는
것입니다. 만약에 징부가 이러한 공류의 지원을 제공한다면 젊은 신혼 부부들이 아이를
가질거라 생각합니다.

Health

Health is something that most people value highly in their lives.

Case 1 **How do you take care of your health?**

I take care of my health by going to the gym twice every week. I go once during the week and once during the weekend. Another thing I do to take care of my health is to make sure I get enough sleep. I've read that sleep deprivation is often the most neglected health problem in Korea.

Case 2 **Do you live a healthy life?**

No, I don't think I live a very healthy life. I smoke as well as drink. Moreover, I eat junk food all the time and I hardly exercise. In addition, I work very long hours and have a lot of stress.

Case 3 **Why is your health important to you?**

My father always tells me that as we age, health becomes the most important thing to maintain and i think I agree with him. Health is important for an enjoyable retirement. When you get older, you can either live a healthy retirement or you can suffer many health conditions and be in constant pain.

Case 4 **Would you rather work out or diet?**

I would much rather diet because I don't like to strain my body with heavy workouts. It's much easier for me to control what I put in my mouth as opposed to lifting a dumbbell or jogging for 30 minutes. Furthermore, I can't stand sweating.

Case 5 **Do you think you are fit?**

Yes, I think I am relatively fit for my age. I'm almost 50 now but I can still jog five kilometers. I've made sure to take care of my body when i was younger and I still exercise every day by walking in the morning. I usually go for a 30 minute walk before I head off to work.

Health

대부분의 사람들이 삶에 있어서 건강을 가장 높은 가치로 두고 있다.

Case 1 당신은 건강관리를 어떻게 하십니까?

매주 2회씩 헬스장에 가서 건강관리를 합니다. 한 번은 주중에 가고 한 번은 주말에 갑니다. 건강관리를 하는 다른 부분은 잠을 충분히 자는 것입니다. 한국인들이 가장 방치하고 있는 건강관리 문제가 수면부족이라고 읽었습니다.

Case 2 당신은 건강한 삶을 살고 있습니까?

아니요. 저는 건강한 삶을 살고 있지 않습니다. 흡연도 하고 있고 음주도 하고 있습니다. 더 나아가 매일 정크푸드를 먹고 운동을 거의 하지 않습니다. 게다가 매우 긴 시간 일을 하면서 스트레스도 많이 받고 있습니다.

Case 3 건강이 왜 당신에게 중요합니까?

우리 아버지는 항상 저에게 아버지 나이가 되면 건강 유지가 가장 중요하다고 말해 주셨습니다. 저 또한 그의 의견에 동의합니다. 건강은 즐거운 은퇴생활을 위해 매우 중요합니다. 나중에 나이가 들면 건강한 은퇴생활을 하거나 건강문제로 고통받으며 계속 아픔속에 살수도 있기때 문입니다.

Case 4 건강관리를 위해 운동과 다이어트중 어느것을 하시겠습니까?

저는 다이어트 하는 것이 더 좋습니다. 왜냐하면 무거운 운동으로 몸을 사용하는것을 좋아하지 않습니다. 먹는것을 조절하는 것이 아령을 들어올리거나 30분 조깅을 하는것보다 훨씬 쉽기 때문입니다. 더 나아가 저는 땀흘리는것을 싫어해요.

Case 5 당신생각에 당신은 건강한가요?

네, 저는 제 나이에 맞게 건강하다고 생각합니다. 저는 거의 50살이지만 아직 5킬로는 뛸수 있습니다. 제가 젊었을때 저를 위해서 많이 단련을 했었고 지금도 매일 아침에 걸으면서 운동을 하고 있습니다. 보통 매일 30분 걷는 운동을 하고 출근합니다.

SPA In-Depth
Part 4

Grammar & Common Error
Focus on: Accuracy / Structure

Question Categories:
 - Hypothetical / Role-play Scenario
 - Making a Decision
 - Making a List
 - Best / Worst, Most / Least
 - Advantages / Disadvantages
 - Have you ever ?

Part 4: Grammar & Common Errors

Preview

Q4 What would you do if your child doesn't want to go to college?

Follow up

How did you feel about college growing up?

Follow up

Do you think it's possible to become successful without having a college degree?

Overview

- Part 4의 배점은 24점이다.
- 문법의 정확도와 문장구성에 대해서 점수 채점이 이루어진다.
- Grammar (parts of speech, verb tenses)와 Structure (syntax, sentence variety / complexity, transitional phrases)를 중심으로 학습을 한다..

Tip

- 다양한 문장 구조를 갖는 것이 높은 점수를 얻는 비결이다.
  간단하고 복잡한 문장을 섞어서 대답을 하도록 연습해보자.
- 접속사를 올바르게 사용하는 것이 높은 점수를 얻을 수 있다.
  올바른 시제 사용에 주의할 것!(과거, 현재, 미래, 과거분사 등)
- 평가위원의 질문에 맞추어 올바른 시제를 사용하여 대답하여야 한다.
- 평소에 생각해보지 않았던 주제에 대한 질문이 자주 나오게 되니 평소에 다양한 토픽에 대해서 준비하고 생각해보도록 해야 한다.

Focus On: Accuracy / Structure

Sample

Part 4 Question | **What would you do if your child doesn't want to go to college?**

Response | If my child doesn't want to go to college, I would ask him what he plans to do instead. If he can convince me that he has a well thought out plan for his life, then I would support his decision.

Follow up #1 | **What if he can't convince you?**

Response | If he can't convince me, then I would have to tell him he can either go to college or lose my financial support. Moreover, he will have to find a new place to live.

Follow up #2 | **Do you think it's possible to become successful without having a college degree?**

Response | I think it's possible but it's a lot harder these days than it was in the past. My father was a success and he never received a college degree. However, back in his time, a college degree wasn't as common as it is now. Since so many people have bachelors degrees nowadays, it's difficult to even get a job with a BA.

Part 4: Grammar & Common Errors

Q4 What would you do if your child doesn't want to go to college?

만약에 당신의 자녀가 대학에 가고 싶지 않다고 하면 어떻게 하시겠습니까?

Response

If my child doesn't want to go to college, I would ask him what he plans to do instead. If he can convince me that he has a well thought out plan for his life, then I would support his decision.

만약에 제 자식이 대학에 가길 원하지 않는다면 대신에 무엇을 하고 싶은지 물어볼 것입니다. 만약에 저를 설득시킬수 있는 계획을 가지고 있다면 제 자식의 의견을 존중하고 지지할 것입니다.

Strategy

- Part 4의 대부분의 질문들이 조건부 질문이다.

조건부 질문은 보통 if, Could, Would, Should로 물어보게 되므로 대답할때도 반드시 질문에서 나오는 문법 시제에 맞추어서 대답하도록 한다.

Example

Q: What **could** Korea do to increase tourism?

A: Korea **could** improve tourism by building a large amusement park.

Q: **If** you **could** travel anywhere in the world, where **would** you go?

A: **If** I **could** travel anywhere in the world, I **would** go to Antartica to see the penguins.

Focus On: Accuracy / Structure

Follow up Q #1   What if he can't convince you?

만약에 당신의 자녀가 당신을 설득 못한다면요?

Response   If he can't convince me, then I would have to tell him he can either go to college or lose my financial support. Moreover, he would have to find a new place to live.

만약에 저를 설득 못한다면 대학에 가던지 부모의 경제적 지원을 포기하던지 선택하라고 하겠습니다. 더불어 독립해서 살 집도 알아보라고 할 것입니다.

Note

- 추가적인 질문은 조건부 상황에서 나오는 시제 형식이 나오기 때문에 대답도 이에 따라 문법적으로 맞추어 대답해야 한다.

- 문장 구성시에 접속사를 적절히 활용하여 대답하면 크게 점수를 올릴 수 있습니다.

- Conjunctions (page 229)를 참고하여 연습해보도록 하세요.

Part 4: Grammar & Common Errors

Follow up Q #2   Do you think it's possible to become successful without having a college degree?

학사 학위 없이 성공적인 삶을 살 수 있을 거라 생각합니까?

Response   I think it's possible but it's a lot harder these days than it was in the past. My father was a success and he never received a college degree. However, back in his time, a college degree wasn't as common as it is now. Since so many people have bachelors degrees nowadays, it's difficult to even get a job with a BA.

학사 학위 없이도 성공적인 삶을 살 수 있을 것 같습니다. 그러나 과거보다는 요즘시대에 좀 더 어려운 것은 사실입니다. 저희 아버지의 경우에도 학사 학위는 없지만 성공적인 삶을 사셨습니다. 그러나 그 당시에는 지금과 비교해서 학사 학위를 따는 것이 흔치 않기도 했습니다. 현재에는 많은 사람들이 학사학위를 따기 때문에 학사 학위가 있어도 직업을 얻기는 마찬가지로 어렵습니다.

Strategy

- 위의 예시는 평가위원이 개인에게 물어보는 전형적인 추가질문이다.

- 일반적인 질문보다 쉽게 대답할수 있는 개인적인 질문을 추가적으로 물어봄으로서 당신이 답변할수 있는 내용을 최대한 끌어내어 수준을 평가하는 것이다.

- 위의 답변을 자세히 살펴보면 화자는 문장간 이어주는 접속사와 화제전환 문구를 잘 사용하였다.

- 다음 페이지에서 단지 접속사 추가만으로 문장 구성이 얼마나 자연스럽게 되는지 비교를 해보고 확인해보도록 한다.

- 접속사 하나로 문장 구성 부분의 점수가 향상 가능하다.

Focus On: Accuracy / Structure

Practice

Do you think it's possible to become successful without having a college degree?

Low score	No, it it's not possible. Companies these days don't hire people without a college degree.
High score	No, it's not possible because companies these days don't hire people without a college degree.
Low score	Yes, it's possible. You can be lucky. You can win the lottery. You can win in black jack.
High score	Yes, it's possible if you are lucky. Perhaps if you win the lottery or win in black jack.
Low score	I think so. It is not easy though. You have to work hard. You have to have a talent for something. You can't be lazy. That is the most important thing.
High score	I think so but it's not easy. You have to work hard and you also have to have a talent for something. Most importantly, you can't be lazy.
Low score	It's possible. My friend is successful. He didn't graduate from college. He has rich parents.
High score	It's possible. My friend is successful and he didn't graduate from college. However, he does have rich parents.

Part 4: Grammar & Common Errors

Hypothetical / Roleplay Scenario

Case 1 — What would you do if your company ordered you to relocate to a different country?

....

....

Case 2 — If you won the jackpot in tomorrow's lottery, what would you do?

....

....

Case 3 — Your close friend had an emergency and asked you if you could lend him some money. What would you do?

....

....

Case 4 — You worked hard all day and it's almost time to go home. At the last moment, your boss asks you to stay an extra hour to help prepare a document. What would you do?

....

....

Case 5 — A relative is trying to find a job in your city and has asked you if he can stay at your home until he finds a job. What would you do?

....

....

Focus On: Accuracy / Structure

Making a Decision

Case 1   Would you rather have a son or daughter?

....

....

Case 2   If you could choose between being 10 years old or 20 years old, which age would you choose and why?

....

....

Case 3   Would you rather diet or exercise?

....

....

Case 4   Where would you rather visit, Paris or New York?

....

....

Case 5   If you could play either the piano or the guitar, which would you choose?

....

....

Part 4: Grammar & Common Errors

Making a List

Case 1　What are some effective ways children can use their cellphones for education?

....

....

Case 2　If you're planning to travel abroad for a year, what are some things you should prepare?

....

....

Case 3　What are some good ways foreigners living in Korea can improve their Korean language skills?

....

....

Case 4　What are some things you can do to stand out as an excellent employee?

....

....

Case 5　What are some simple changes you can make to improve your overall health?

....

....

Focus On: Accuracy / Structure

Best / Worst, Most / Least

Case 1   What is the best job in Korea?

....

....

Case 2   What is the worst thing about living in your city?

....

....

Case 3   What is the most important life lesson you would pass onto your children?

....

....

Case 4   What is the most useful product that you own?

....

....

Case 5   There are many factors to consider when choosing a career. What do you think are the most important things to consider?

....

....

Advantages / Disadvantages

Case 1   What are some of the advantages and disadvantages of having a large family?

....

....

Case 2   What are some of the advantages and disadvantages of studying abroad?

....

....

Case 3   What are some positive and negative aspects of the internet?

....

....

Case 4   What are the advantages of being the youngest child? Are there any disadvantages?

....

....

Case 5   What are the advantages and disadvantages of working in a small company compared to working in a large company?

....

....

Focus On: Accuracy / Structure

Have you ever?

Case 1　　Have you ever met someone famous in person before? If not, who would you want to meet?

　　　　　　..

　　　　　　..

Case 2　　Have you ever considered starting your own business? If not, what kind of business would you be good at running?

　　　　　　..

　　　　　　..

Case 3　　Have you ever lost your cellphone? If not, what would you do if you lost your cellphone?

　　　　　　..

　　　　　　..

Case 4　　Have you ever been to a concert? If not, what concert would you like to go to?

　　　　　　..

　　　　　　..

Case 5　　Have you ever experienced culture shock? If not, what do you think would be the biggest shock to you if you traveled abroad?

　　　　　　..

　　　　　　..

Part 4 Practice

Hypothetical / Roleplay Scenario

Case 1 — **What would you do if your company ordered you to relocate to a different country?**

If my company asked me to relocate to a different country, I would definitely consider it. However, I'd have to consider how long I would have to stay there. Furthermore, my decision would be highly dependent on what region I was relocating too. If it was a developed region like Europe or America, I think I'd be more willing to go.

Case 2 — **If you won the jackpot in tomorrow's lottery, what would you do?**

If I won tomorrow's jackpot, I wouldn't change too many things about my life. I'd buy my family a few nice presents and save the rest of the money for retirement. I would want to keep my job because I have heard of stories where people who won the lottery quickly spent all their money and ended up broke.

Case 3 — **Your close friend had an emergency and asked you if you could lend him some money. What would you do?**

I would lend him a little bit of money if he really needed it but I don't think I could lend him a lot. It's always risky lending people money, especially if they are close to you.

Case 4 — **You worked hard all day and it's almost time to go home. At the last moment, your boss asks you to stay an extra hour to help prepare a document. What would you do?**

When I was younger, I would probably stay and help. However, as I've aged, I've learned that my personal time is more important than fixing other people's problems at work.

Case 5 — **A relative is trying to find a job in your city and has asked you if he can stay at your home until he finds a job. What would you do?**

I would tell him to first look online for jobs in my city before moving into my house. If he can secure a few interviews, then he would be more than welcome to stay at my house for a short while. However, I would be very clear on exactly how long he can stay at my house.

Focus On: Accuracy / Structure

Hypothetical / Roleplay Scenario

Case 1　만약에 당신의 회사가 당신에게 해외 근무 발령을 내리면 어떻게 하겠습니까?

만약에 회사가 저에게 다른 나라 파견근무 지시를 한다면 당연히 가도록 하겠지만 얼마나 오랫동안 머물러야 하는지 고려해봐야 할 것이며, 또한 어느 장소로 가게 되느냐에 따라도 결정이 달라질수도 있을 것 같습니다. 유럽이나 미국같이 발전된 곳이면 가는 것을 결정할 것 같습니다.

Case 2　만약에 당신이 로또 1등에 당첨되면 어떻게 하시겠습니까?

만약에 내가 로또 1등에 당첨된다면 저는 제 삶에 대해서 많은 것을 바꾸지는 않을 것입니다. 가족들에게 좋은 선물을 해주고 은퇴이후를 위해 저금을 해놓겠습니다. 직장은 계속 다니고 싶습니다. 왜냐하면 로또에 담첨되고 돈을 흥청망청 다 써서 파산하는 사례를 많이 들었거든요.

Case 3　당신의 친한 친구가 긴급하게 당신에게 돈을 빌려달려고 요청한다면 어떻게 하시겠습니까?

만약에 친구가 진짜 필요하다면 어느정도는 빌려줄수 있을것입니다. 그러나 큰 돈은 빌려줄 수 없습니다. 누군가에게 돈을 빌려주는 것은 항상 위험부담이 있으니까요. 특히 가까운 사람한테는요.

Case 4　당신은 하루종일 일을 열심히 했고 거의 퇴근시간이 되었다. 그 순간 당신의 상사가 서류준비를 위해 야근을 지시하면 어떻게 하시겠습니까?

회사에 갓 들어갔을때는 아마도 야근해서 도와주었을 것 같은데 그러나 지금 어느정도 경력이 쌓였고 내 개인 시간이 다른 사람의 일을 도와주는 것보다 중요하다는 것을 배웠기 때문에 상사의 요청을 거절할 것입니다.

Case 5　당신의 친척이 당신이 살고있는 도시에서 직업을 찾으려고 합니다. 그리고 당신의 집에서 머물러도 되냐고 물어본다면 어떻게 하시겠습니까?

우리집으로 이사오기전에 우선 온라인에서 직장을 찾아보고 오라고 말 할 것입니다. 만약에 몇개의 확실한 면접이 있다고 하면 얼마동안 우리집에 머무르는 것은 괜찮을 것 같습니다.다. 따라서 친척이 우리집에 얼마동안 머무르게 될 것인지를 확실하게 정리하고 싶습니다.

Part 4: Grammar & Common Errors

Making a Decision

Case 1 — **Would you rather have a son or daughter?**

I would be happy with either a son or daughter. However, if I really had to choose between the two, I would say daughter because girls tend to behave a little better than boys at a young age.

Case 2 — **If you could choose between being 10 years old or 20 years old, which age would you choose and why?**

If I had to choose, I'd pick being 20 years old. The reason I'd pick 20 is because at that age, you still have the freedom of being an adult. Also, I wouldn't want to go through high school all over again.

Case 3 — **Would you rather diet or exercise?**

I would rather exercise because I love eating too much. In addition, exercising is a lot more social. For example, I can play basketball with my friends or go to the gym with my gym partner. If I diet, I can't enjoy going to restaurants with my friends.

Case 4 — **Where would you rather visit, Paris or New York?**

I would rather visit Paris because it's got a lot more history than New York. I would love to see the Palace of Versailles or the Eiffel Tower.

Case 5 — **If you could play either the piano or the guitar, which would you choose?**

If I could choose one instrument, I would choose the guitar because it's a more trendy instrument. Most of the popular musicians these days play the guitar rather than the piano so I'd also want to play the guitar.

Focus On: Accuracy / Structure

Making a Decision

Case 1   딸과 아들중 어떤쪽을 원하십니까?

저는 딸이건 아들이건 상관없이 행복할 것 같습니다. 그러나 어쩔수 없이 둘중에 하나를 고르라고 하면 딸을 갖고 싶습니다. 왜냐하면 어렸을때는 여자아이가 남자아이보다 더 말을 잘 듣기 때문입니다.

Case 2   만약에 당신이 10대 혹은 20대로 돌아갈수 있다면 어떤 나이대로 돌아가고 싶습니까?

저는 20대로 돌아가는 것을 선택하겠습니다. 20대를 선택한 이유는 성인으로서의 자유를 가지고 있기 때문이며 또한 다시 고등학교로 돌아가고 싶지 않기 때문이기도 합니다.

Case 3   살을 빼기 위해 다이어트와 운동중 어느 것을 선택하겠습니까?

저는 운동을 선택하겠습니다. 이유는 저는 먹는것을 너무 좋아하기 때문입니다. 게다가 운동은 사회적인 활동이기 때문입니다. 예를들어 농구하러 친구랑 가거나 헬스장에도 동료와 갈 수 있습니다. 만약에 제가 다이어트를 한다면 친구들과 레스토랑에 가서 맛있는 음식을 먹을수 없기에 다이어트는 선택하지 않을 것입니다.

Case 4   파리와 뉴욕중에 어느 도시를 방문하고 싶습니까?

저는 파리에 가는것이 더 좋습니다. 뉴욕보다 더 역사적인 장소이기 때문입니다. 베르샤유 궁전과 에펠타워도 보고 싶습니다.

Case 5   피아노와 기타 중 어느 것을 연주하고 싶습니까?

한개의 악기를 선택하라고 하면 기타를 선택하겠습니다. 다른 악기보다 트렌디한 악기이기 때문입니다. 오늘날 유명한 뮤지션들은 모두 피아노보다는 기타를 연주합니다. 그렇기 때문에 기타를 연주해보고 싶습니다.

Part 4: Grammar & Common Errors

Making a List

Case 1 — **What are some effective ways children can use their cellphones for education?**

There are some great educational apps available for free download. I think the problem, however, lies in all the other non-educational programs also available to distract children from learning. If parents can control access to things like games and chatting, I think smartphones can become a viable source of education.

Case 2 — **If you're planning to travel abroad for a year, what are some things you should prepare?**

I think the most important thing for me to prepare would be my laptop. I wouldn't be able to survive without having access to my emails and online chatting. Next, I'd probably prepare about two weeks worth of clothes. Lastly, I would try and say goodbye to all of my friends and family before I left.

Case 3 — **How can foreigners living in Korea improve their Korean skills?**

For one, they could try to take some Korean classes. A lot of classes are sponsored by the Korean government so it's free for anyone that wants to learn Korean. Another thing they could do is try and meet some Korean friends. Having native friends to practice can really help a lot. Moreover, they could start reading the newspaper in the morning.

Case 4 — **What are some things you can do to stand out as an excellent employee?**

The first thing that comes to my mind is to always be early to work. If you're always in your office before everyone else, your boss might see you as someone who works hard and cares about his work. Furthermore, you could stand out by always having a positive attitude.

Case 5 — **What are some simple changes you can make to improve your overall health?**

A simple thing I could do to improve my health is to not eat late at night. Another thing I could do is to use the stairs instead of the elevator. Lastly, I could skip dessert.

Focus On: Accuracy / Structure
Making a List

Case 1 아이들이 자신의 휴대폰을 교육용으로 사용할 수 있는 효과적인 방법들은 무엇이 있습니까?

스마트폰에는 무료로 다운로드 받을수 있는 훌륭한 앱들이 있습니다. 문제는 다른 비교육적인 프로그램들이 아이들 학습하는데 방해가 될수도 있는 점 입니다. 만약에 부모님이 모바일 게임이나 채팅 같은것을 컨트롤 해줄 수 있다면 스마트폰은 교육의 좋은 원천이 될수 있을 것입니다.

Case 2 만약에 당신이 1년동안 해외 여행을 계획하고 있다면 준비해야 할 물건들은 무엇이 있습니까?

저에게 가장 중요한 것은 노트북 을 준비해가는 것입니다. 이메일과 온라인 채팅 없이는 살 수가 없을것 같습니다. 다음으로는 2주정도의 옷을 준비하고 마지막으로 떠나기 전에 친구들과 가족들에게 작별인사를 할 것입니다.

Case 3 외국인이 한국에 살면서 어떻게 한국어 능력을 올릴수 있을까요?

첫 번째로 한국어 수업을 듣는 것을 시도해 보아야 합니다. 한국 정부가 무료로 많은 수업들을 후원을 해주고 있기 때문에 쉽게 한국어를 배울 수 있습니다. 한국인 친구를 사귀어 보는것도 좋은 시도입니다. 한국인 친구와 연습하면 한국어 연습에 큰 도움이 됩니다. 이외에 아침에 한국 신문을 읽어보는 것도 도움이 됩니다.

Case 4 당신이 훌륭한 직원으로 눈에 띄게 하기 위해서는 무엇이 필요할까요?

첫 번째로 생각나는 것이 일찍 출근을 하는 것입니다. 만약에 매 번 가장 먼저 출근을 하게 된다면 당신의 상사는 당신이 좀더 열심히 일하고 일에 노력을 많이 한다고 생각할 것입니다.
더 나아가 항상 긍정적인 태도를 가지고 있으면 눈에 띄일 수 있습니다.

Case 5 당신의 전반적인 건강을 개선하기 위해 할 수 있는 몇 가지 간단한 변화는 무엇인가요?

간단하게 내 건강을 챙기는 방법은 밤 늦게 밥을 먹지 않는 것입니다. 또 다른 방법은 엘리베이터 사용 대신에 계단을 이용하는 것이 있고 마지막으로 디저트류를 먹지 않는 것이 있습니다.

Best / Worst, Most / Least

Case 1 — **What is the best job in Korea?**

The best job in Korea is to work as a government worker. The reason for this is because they have the most job security. Furthermore, government workers get paid well considering the amount of work they do.

Case 2 — **What is the worst thing about living in your city?**

The worst thing about living in my city is the traffic. The roads in Ulsan are very old and narrow so during rush hour, it can take a very long time to go to work or go home. This condition is further escalated by the lack of mass transit like a subway system.

Case 3 — **What is the most important life lesson you would pass onto your children?**

The most important life lesson I'd pass onto my children is to never give up on your dreams. You only have one life to live so you should live it the way you want to.

Case 4 — **What is the most useful product that you own?**

The most useful product that I own would have to be my cellphone. I use it for almost everything including entertainment, productivity, communication, and taking pictures. I've gotten so used to using it for everything that I can't imagine my life without it.

Case 5 — **There are many factors to consider when choosing a career. What do you think are the most important things to consider?**

I believe the most important thing to consider when choosing a career path is to consider what you're truly good at. If you are better at something than most people, you can make money off of it. Some people may say choose a career that makes you happy, but happiness doesn't always pay the bills.

Best / Worst, Most / Least

Case 1 한국에서 최고의 직업은 무엇입니까?

한국에서 최고의 직업은 공무원입니다. 이유는 가장 안정적인 직업이기 때문입니다. 더 나아가 공무원은 총 근무시간에 맞추어 월급이 주어지기 때문에 좋은 직업이라고 생각합니다.

Case 2 당신의 도시에서 살면서 최악인 것은 무엇입니까?

우리도시에서 사는것 중 최악인 것은 교통입니다. 울산의 도로는 매우 오래되었고 좁기때문에 출퇴근시간이 되면 차가 매우 막힙니다. 지하철과 같은 커다란 대중 교통이 없기 때문에 항상 교통체증이 있습니다.

Case 3 당신의 아이에게 전해줄 수 있는 가장 중요한 인생교훈은 무엇입니까?

내가 자식에게 줄 수 있는 최고의 인생교훈은 꿈에 대하여 포기하지 말라는 것입니다. 한 번 밖에 살지 않는 인생이기 때문에 원하는 것을 위해 살아야 한다고 가르치고 싶습니다.

Case 4 당신이 가지고 있는 물건중 가장 유용한 물건은 무엇입니까?

내가 가지고 있는 물건 중 가장 유용한 제품은 휴대폰입니다. 저는 휴대폰으로 엔터테인먼트, 생산적인 일, 커뮤니케이션, 사진찍기등 거의 모든것에 대해 사용합니다. 저는 휴대폰에 너무 익숙해져있어서 휴대폰 없는 삶은 상상할 수 없습니다.

Case 5 직업을 선택할때 많은 부분을 고려할 수 있습니다. 가장 중요하게 고려해야 할 부분은 무엇입니까?

나는 진로를 결정할때 가장 중요하게 생각하는 것은 내가 진짜 잘하는 것이 무엇인지 고려하는 것입니다. 만약에 당신이 일반사람보다 무엇인가 더 잘한다면 그것으로도 돈을 벌 수 있습니다. 어떤 사람들은 당신이 행복한 직업을 구하라고 조언하지만 행복이 항상 돈을 가져오는 것은 아닙니다.

Advantages / Disadvantages

Case 1 — **What are some of the advantages and disadvantages of having a large family?**

One of the advantages of having a large family is having a large number of people who care for your well being. If you're in need of help, there will be many people who can help you. Consequently, that advantage can also be a disadvantage. Sometimes, you could be overwhelmed by the amount of people who are constantly checking up on you.

Case 2 — **What are some of the advantages and disadvantages of studying abroad?**

Studying abroad can be a great way to learn about a different culture in-depth. Aside from the things you learn on campus, you can learn a tremendous amount about life in general just by living in a different setting than what you're accustomed to. I think the only real disadvantage is not being close to your friends or family while you're away.

Case 3 — **What are some positive and negative aspects of the internet?**

Being able to access an almost limitless amount of information is a huge advantage of having the internet. With advanced search engines like google or naver, finding whatever information you are looking for is extremely easy. On the other hand, because there's so much information that's readily available online, privacy can become a major concern.

Case 4 — **What are the advantages of being the youngest child? Are there any disadvantages?**

I think the biggest advantage to being the youngest child is that you have older siblings who will take care of you and help you with things like school work. In addition, a lot of parents seem to go a lot easier on the youngest. On the flip side, you'll probably often receive hand-me-downs rather than new items.

Case 5 — **What are the advantages and disadvantages of working in a small company compared to working in a large company?**

Since I've never worked for a small company, I can't really share my own experiences. However, I'd imagine it to be a lot more stressful than working for a large company because of the uncertainty of not knowing if the company will survive or not. If the company fails, you lose your job so that is something you never really want to worry about. I suppose an advantage might be that you could have more opportunity to impact your company and advance faster up the corporate ladder.

Advantages / Disadvantages

Focus On: Accuracy / Structure

Case 1   대가족의 장단점들은 무엇입니까?

대가족의 장점은 당신을 도와 줄 많은 숫자의 가족들이 있다는 것입니다. 만약에 당신이 도움이 필요하면 많은 가족들이 당신을 도와 줄 수 있을 것입니다. 결과적으로 이러한 장점은 양날의 검이 될 수도 있습니다. 때때로 많은 사람들이 당신을 지속적으로 체크하고 간섭할 수 있기도 합니다.

Case 2   해외유학의 장단점은 무엇입니까?

해외 유학은 다른 문화를 깊게 배울 수 있는 최고의 방법입니다. 캠퍼스에서 배운것을 떠나 당신이 익숙한 환경과 다른 곳에서 살아보면서 여러가지 삶을 경험하고 배울수 있습니다. 단점이라면 오직 가족과 친구들과 멀리 떨어져 지낸다는 점인것 같습니다.

Case 3   인터넷의 긍정적인 면과 부정적인 면은 무엇입니까?

거의 제한없는 양의 정보를 접할수 있다는 것이 인터넷 사용의 장점입니다. 구글이나 네이버 같은 검색엔진을 이용하면 당신이 원하는 정보 검색은 매우 쉬워집니다. 반대로 말하면 온라인으로 접근할수 있는 정보가 너무 많기 때문에 개인 정보 보호가 주요 관심사가 될 수 있습니다.

Case 4   가족에서 막내로서의 장점은 무엇일까요? 단점도 있을까요?

막내의 가장 큰 장점은 당신을 보살펴 주고 학교 숙제같은 것을 도와줄 수 있는 형,누나가 있는 것입니다. 또한 대부분의 부모들은 막내를 더 귀엽게 생각합니다. 그러나 다른 측면으로 막내는 항상 새로운 물건보다는 물려받는 물건이 더 많을 것입니다.

Case 5   대기업과 비교해서 작은회사에서 일하는 장단점은 무엇입니까?

작은 회사에서 한 번도 일해본 경험이 없기 때문에 내 경험을 비교해서 말할수는 없지만 아마도 대기업에서 일하는 것보다 스트레스가 더 많을 것으로 상상이 됩니다. 왜냐하면 회사가 계속해서 살아남을 수 있는지 불확실하기 때문입니다. 만약에 회사가 망하면 당신은 직장을 잃기 때문에 회사의 불확실성은 정말 걱정하고 싶지 않은 부분일것입니다. 작은 회사에서의 장점이라면 아마도 회사에 영향을 끼칠 좋은 기회들이 많고 더 빠르게 승진할 수 있는 것일 것입니다.

Part 4: Grammar & Common Errors

Have you ever?

Case 1 **Have you ever met someone famous in person before? If not, who would you want to meet?**

Yes, I once walked by Jun Ji Hyun while I was in college. She happened to attend my university when I was a student there. I couldn't believe my eyes. She looked even better in person than on TV.

Case 2 **Have you ever considered starting your own business? If not, what kind of business would you be good at running?**

Yes, I have. However, I never took the initiative to get the ball rolling. There is simply too many things to worry about like hiring the right people, find a good office location, and contacting clients. After about a day of seriously contemplating it, I decided I'm not the entrepreneur type.

Case 3 **Have you ever lost your cellphone? If not, what would you do if you lost your cellphone?**

No, I have never lost my cellphone. Luckily, I have an iPhone so if I ever lose it, I can access my phone's gps via my computer and find out where it is. In addition, I can also remote lock my phone so that other people won't have access to my personal data.

Case 4 **Have you ever been to a concert? If not, what concert would you like to go to?**

No, I have never been to a concert. I'm just not that interested in music. I suppose if I were to go to a concert, it would probably be a Rolling Stones concert. I heard they have amazing performances.

Case 5 **Have you ever experienced culture shock? If not, what do you think would be the biggest shock to you if you traveled abroad?**

Yes, when I was traveling through America, I experienced quite a bit of culture shock. For starters, I was surprised that Americans walk around with their shoes on while inside their homes. Another thing that I wasn't used to was how so many people wear shorts and slippers.

Focus On: Accuracy / Structure

Have you ever?

Case 1   유명한 사람과 개인적으로 만나본적이 있습니까? 없다면 누구를 만나보고 싶습니까?

대학다닐때 전지현을 본적이 있습니다. 대학생이었을때 전지현이 우리학교에 들어왔고 내눈을 믿을수가 없었습니다. 실제로 보면 TV보다 더 예쁩니다.

Case 2   창업을 고려해본적이 있습니까? 만약에 없다면 어떤 비즈니스 분야의 창업이 잘 될 것 같습니까?

네 있습니다. 그러나 계획적으로 일을 진행 해본 적은 없습니다. 창업에는 사람을 뽑고 사무실을 구하고 고객들과 연락하고 많은 일들을 걱정해야 하는 부분이 있습니다. 하루정도 심각하게 고민을 해보고 나는 기업가 스타일이 아니라고 결정 내렸습니다.

Case 3   휴대폰을 잃어버려 본 적이 있습니까? 만약에 없다면 잃어버렸을 경우 어떻게 하시겠습니까?

한 번도 휴대폰을 잃어버려 본 적이 없습니다. 운 좋게도 저는 아이폰을 갖고 있는데 만약에 잃어 버리면 내 핸드폰의 GPS를 컴퓨터로 접속하여 어디에 있는지 찾아낼 수 있습니다. 게다가 무선으로 휴대폰을 잠글수도 있습니다. 그래서 다른 사람들이 내 개인 정보를 볼 수가 없습니다.

Case 4   콘서트장에 가본적이 있습니까? 없다면 어떤 콘서트장에 가보고 싶습니까?

저는 콘서트장에 한번도 가 본 적이 없습니다. 그냥 음악에 그렇게 관심이 없습니다. 간다고 가정했을때 저는 롤링스톤 콘서트장에 가보고 싶습니다. 롤링스톤의 퍼포먼스가 훌륭하다고 들었기 때문입니다.

Case 5   문화충격을 받아본적이 있습니까? 만약에 없다면 해외여행중에 어떠한 것이 가장 큰 문화충격일 것 같습니까?

미국을 여행했을때 문화충격을 받은적이 있습니다. 우선 첫째로 미국인들이 집안에서 신발을 신고 돌아다니는 것이 깜짝놀랐습니다. 또 놀란 점은 많은 사람들이 짧은 반바지에 슬리퍼 신고 돌아다니는 것이 익숙하지 않았습니다.

SPA In-Depth
Part 5

Overall Fluency
Focus on: Confidence / Logic

Question Categories:
 - Description
 - Bar Graph
 - Pie Graph
 - Line Graph
 - Role Play
 - Preference

Part 5: Overall Fluency

Preview

Q5 Describe what is happening in this picture. What do you think will happen next?

Overview

- Part 5의 배점은 12점이다.
- Part 5는 사진을 묘사하거나 사진과 관련된 질문에 대답하여야 합니다
- 사진이외에 또한 그래프, 챠트, 롤플레이, 두개의 사진 비교하기 문제 유형이 있다.
- 언어구사능력 (Overall Fluency)에 대해 채점을 하게된다.
- 자신감, 논리적인 전개, 묘사력 그리고 자연스럽게 원하는 것을 표현 하는 능력에 대해 채점이 이루어진다.

Tip

- Part 5에서는 추가질문이 거의 이루어지지 않는다. 그이유는 간단하다.
  시험 시간이 10분으로 제한되어 있기 때문에 마지막 질문에 추가 질문의 여유가 없다.
  (간혹 시간이 모자를 경우 Part 5는 아예 물어보지 않는 경우도 있다.).
  평가위원은 앞선 질문만으로도 이미 당신의 일반적인 말하기 능력 수준을 잡아낼 수 있다.

Focus On: Confidence / Logic

Sample

Q5 Describe what is happening in this picture. What do you think will happen next?

Response This is a picture of a <u>car accident</u>. It looks like a pretty <u>serious</u>
　　　　　　　　　　　　　　　　　main　　　　　　　　　　　　　　　　　　　　　assumption
<u>accident</u> because <u>the bumpers on both cars came off</u>. There
　　　　　　　　　　　　　　　　detail
are <u>three men gathered</u> around the accident. Based on the
　　　　detail
<u>vests</u> they are wearing It looks like they are <u>either police</u>
detail
<u>officers or maybe mechanics</u>. <u>I hope the people involved in</u>
　　　　assumption　　　　　　　　　　　　　　feelings / thoughts
<u>the accident weren't seriously injured</u>. I think that what will happen is that the two car owners will exchange insurance information. If they were injured in the accident, they may head to the hospital.

Strategy

위에 샘플 답안을 참고하여 정리된 대답을 연습해보도록 한다.

- 사진을 묘사할때는 당신의 답변을 논리있게 정돈하여 대답하는 것이 중요하다.

  1. Main 일반적으로 처음에는 사진의 주요 특징을 묘사를 하며 시작한다
  2. Detail 사진을 분석하거나 가정하는 것을 추가하여 설명한다.
  3. Opinion / Analysis 사진에 대한 당신의 생각이나 느낌을 포함해서 대화를 마무리 한다.

때때로 평가위원은 사진에 관련된 질문을 하게 되는데 이럴때는 질문에 관련하여 답변을 하고 끝마치도록 한다.

SPA 시험에서는 다양한 종류의 사진들이 나오고 있다. 다음 페이지부터는 SPA시험에서 자주 출제되는 형식의 사진 유형들을 연습해 보도록 한다.

Description

Describe what is happening in this picture. Why do you think they are carrying all these instruments?

Practice

There are ....

They are holding ....

It looks like there is ....

They are probably ....

Perhaps they are ....

I can tell that ....

Focus On: Confidence / Logic

Description

There are four men walking on a beach.

They are holding various musical instruments.

It looks like there is a trumpet, a guitar, and a cello.

They are probably some sort of band.

Perhaps they are going to perform on the beach

I can tell that they are in a tropical climate.

Answer

Describe what is happening in this picture.
이 사진에서 어떠한 일이 일어나고 있는지 설명해 보세요.

There are four men walking on a beach. They are holding various musical instruments. It looks like there is a trumpet, a guitar, and a cello. I'm not sure what the second man to the left is holding. They are probably some sort of band, possibly a mariachi. Perhaps they are going to perform on the beach for a special event like a wedding or concert. By the way the sand looks and by the clothes they are wearing, I can tell that they are in a tropical climate.

해변에 네 명의 남자가 걷고 있습니다. 그들은 다양한 악기를 메고 있습니다. 그 악기는 트럼펫, 기타 그리고 첼로인것 같고 두번째 남자가 왼쪽에 갖고 있는것이 무엇인지는 모르겠습니다. 이 사람들은 어떤 밴드인것 같은데 아마도 마리아치 인것 같습니다. 이들은 해변에서 열리는 결혼식이나 콘서트에 연주하러 가는 것 같습니다. 모래와 옷 입은 형태로 보아 그들은 열대기후에 있는 것 같습니다.

Part 5: Overall Fluency

Bar Graph

Please explain what this graph is showing. What are the benefits of having a fast internet connection?

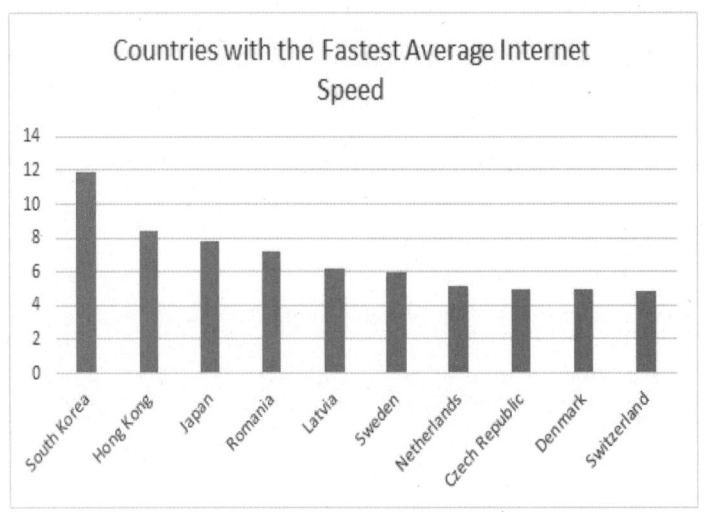

Practice

This graph respresents ....

The top three ....

The remaining ....

Based on this graph, ...

The benefits of having a fast internet are ....

Overall, ...

Focus On: Confidence / Logic

Bar Graph

This graph represents the countries with the fastest average internet speed in the world.

The top three countries are Korea, Hong Kong, and Japan.

The remaining seven countries are all from Europe.

Based on this graph, it seems that the countries witht the fastest internet are all small

The benefits of having a fast internet are faster download speeds and an easier time finding information.

Overall, I believe it has a positive effect on education.

Answer

Please explain what this graph is showing. What are the benefits of having a fast internet connection?
이 그래프가 무엇을 나타내는지 설명해 주세요. 인터넷이 빠르면 어떤 장점이 있을까요?

This graph represents the countries with the fastest average internet speed in the world. The top three countries are all in Asia with Korea in first, Hong Kong in second, and Japan in third. The remaining seven countries are all from Europe. Based on this graph, it seems that the countries with the fastest internet all have a commonality; they're all relatively small in terms of land area.

There's a number of benefits for having a fast internet connection. For starters, finding information online becomes much faster. Downloading and sharing information also becomes faster. Overall, I believe it has a positive effect on education as well as commerce.

이 그래프는 인터넷 평균 속도가 세계에서 가장 빠른 국가들을 나타내고 있다.
탑3 국가는 모두 아시아 국가이고 1위가 한국, 2위가 홍콩, 3위가 일본이다. 남은 7개의 국가는 모두 유럽국가들이다. 그래프에 따르면 인터넷이 빠른 나라들은 모두 공통점이 있는데 그것은 모두 토지 면적이 작은 나라들이라는 것이다.

인터넷이 빠르면 많은 장점들이 있다. 우선 온라인에서 정보를 찾는 것이 훨씬 빨라진다. 전체적으로 이는 교육뿐 아니라 상업적인 면에서도 긍정적인 영향을 미친다.

Pie Graph

Please describe the graph. Which search engine do you prefer and why?

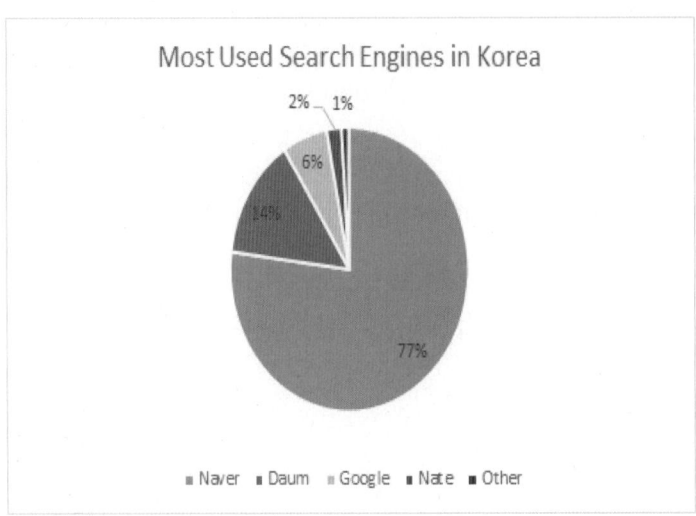

Practice

The graph highlights ....

.... is the most used ....

What I find interesting is ....

I prefer .... because ....

Focus On: Confidence / Logic

Pie Graph

The graph highlights the most used search engines in Korea.

Naver **is the most used** search engine.

What I find interesting is that compared to other countries, Google's market share in Korea is very small.

I prefer to use Naver **because** it's homepage has everything I need.

Answer

Please describe the graph. Which search engine do you prefer and why?
그래프를 설명해주세요. 당신은 어떤 검색엔진을 선호합니까? 이유는요?

The graph highlights the most used search engines in Korea. Naver is by far the most used search engine, accounting for 77% of the market share. Daum is a distant second with 14% of users and Google is next at 6%. What I find interesting about this graph is that compared to other countries, Google's market share in Korea is miniscule.

I prefer to use Naver because its homepage has everything I am looking for, be it news, sports, email, pictures, videos, or shopping. I can do almost anything I want to do easily from their home page.

그래프는 한국에서 가장 많이 사용되는 검색엔진을 표시하였다.
네이버 는 시장 점유율 77 % 를 차지, 지금까지 가장 많이 사용되는 검색 엔진으로 나온다. 차이가 나는 2위로 다음이 14%를 차지하였고 그 다음은 6%의 구글이 차지하였다. 이 그래프에서 재미있는 것은 다른 나라와 비교하여 한국에서의 구글 시장 점유율이 더 적다는 것이다.

저는 네이버 사용을 더 선호합니다. 왜냐하면 홈페이지에 내가 찾는 모든 것들이 있습니다. 이를테면 뉴스, 스포츠, 이메일, 사진, 비디오, 쇼핑 같은 것들이요. 제가 하고 싶은 모든 것들이 홈페이지에서 쉽게 접근 할 수 있어서 네이버를 선호합니다.

Part 5: Overall Fluency

Line Graph

Please explain what this graph is showing. Why do you think this is?

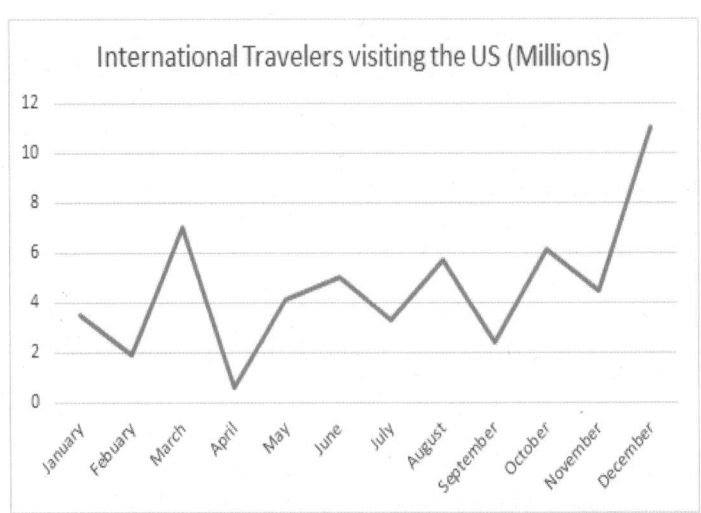

Practice

The graph is showing ....

The most ....

The least ....

I think .... because ....

Focus On: Confidence / Logic

Line Graph

The graph is showing the amount of international travelers visiting the United States each month.

The most visited time of year is December.

The least visited time of year is April.

I think December is the most visited time of year **because** of the holiday season.

Part 5 Practice

Answer

Please explain what this graph is showing. Why do you think this is?
이 그래프가 어떤 것을 보여주는지 설명해 주세요. 왜 이렇게 생각을 하나요?

The graph is showing the amount of international travelers visiting the United States each month. The most visited time of year is December and the least visited time of year is April. I think December is the most visited time of year because of the holiday season. Many people like to travel during the holidays to visit their relatives or to simply enjoy their long vacations.

그래프는 월 별 미국을 방문하는 해외 여행객 총 합을 나타내고 있습니다. 12월에 가장 많은 방문자들이 있었고 4월에 가장 적은 방문사가 있었습니다. 12월이 휴가시즌이기 때문에 가장 많은 방문자가 있는것 같습니다.. 많은 사람들이 휴가시즌에 가족 친척들을 방문하거나 긴 휴가를 즐기기를 원하니까요.

Part 5: Overall Fluency

Role Play

You are trying to sell this house. Convince me why I should buy it.

Practice

This house is ....

Inside, there is ....

Outside, there is ....

This house ....

Focus On: Confidence / Logic

Role Play

This house is perfect for people who want to relax.

Inside, there is a spacious kitchen, a master bedroom, and a living room.

Outside, there is a beautiful front yard with flowers.

This house costs only ten thousand dollars.

Answer

You are trying to sell this house. Convince me why I should buy it.
당신은 이 집을 팔고자 합니다. 내가 왜 이 집을 사야 하는지 설득해보세요.

This quaint little house is the perfect home for people who want to relax and be comfortable at home. Inside, you have everything you could need such as a surprisingly spacious kitchen, a beautiful master bedroom, and a cozy living room. To top it all off, this house even comes with a beautiful front yard which you can use to plant flowers, fruits, and vegetables. All of this is included in the very attractive price of only ten thousand dollars.

이 진귀하고 작은 집은 집에서 편안하게 휴식을 취하고 싶어하는 사람들에게 완벽한 집입니다. 안에는 놀라울 정도로 넓은 부엌 , 아름다운 침실 과 아늑한 거실 로 필요로 하는 모든 것을 갖추고 있습니다. 게다가 이 집 은 심지어 당신이 꽃을 심거나 과일과 채소를 심을 수 있도록 아름다운 앞마당이 함께 제공됩니다. 이 모든 것이 단지 10 만 달러 의 매우 매력적인 가격에 포함되어 있습니다.

Part 5: Overall Fluency

Compare and Contrast

Please describe the following pictures, explaining the similarities and differences between the two.

Practice

The two pictures are ....

In the first picture, ...

In the second picture, ...

One thing that's similar is ....

One thing that's different is ....

Focus On: Confidence / Logic

Compare and Contrast

The two pictures are of two different pairs of shoes.

In the first picture, there is a brown pair of shoes with laces.

In the second picture, there is a black pair of shoes with no laces.

One thing that's similar is that they are both work shoes.

One thing that's different is that one is for working outdoors and one is for working in an office.

Answer

Please describe the following pictures, explaining the similarities and differences between the two.
아래 사진을 묘사하고 두 사진의 비슷한점과 다른 점을 설명해주세요.

The two pictures are of two different pairs of shoes. The first pair is brown and has laces. The second pair is black and does not have any laces on it. They are similar in that they are both work shoes. The difference is that one is for working outdoors and the other one is for working in an office.

두 사진은 다른 형태의 신발 한쌍이다. 첫 번째 신발은 갈색이고 끈이 있습니다.
두 번째 신발은 검정색이고 끈이 없습니다. 비슷한 점은 둘다 작업화 라는 것입니다 다른점은 하나는 밖에서 일할 때 신는 신발이고 하나는 회사안에서 일할때 신는 신발입니다.

Part 5: Overall Fluency

Compare and Contrast

Please describe the following pictures, explaining the advantages and disadvantages of each area. Which area would you prefer to live in?

Practice

The first picture is ....

The second picture is ....

The advantage of ....

The disadvantage of ....

I would prefer to live in ....

Focus On: Confidence / Logic

Compare and Contrast

The first picture is of an urban setting.

The second picture is of a rural setting.

The advantage of urban living is that things are a lot more convenient.

The disadvantage of urban living is that it is too crowded.

I would prefer to live in a rural setting because I enjoy nature.

Answer

Please describe the following pictures, explaining the advantages and disadvantages of each area. Which area would you prefer to live in?
아래 사진을 묘사해 주세요. 각 지역의 장 단점을 설명해주세요. 어느 지역에서 더 살고 싶습니까?

The first picture is of an urban setting. The advantage of living in an urban setting is that things are a lot more convenient. Stores are a lot closer together, and there is a lot more to see and do in a small area. The main disadvantage is that it is usually crowded.

The second picture is of a rural setting. I think the biggest advantage of living in a rural area is the peace and quiet. There's a lot less hustle and bustle so you can generally live a less stressful life. The main disadvantage is the isolation. You will most likely have to travel a greater distance to do anything.

I would prefer to live in a rural setting because I enjoy nature and being alone. Living in a big city can be quite hectic.

첫 번째 사진은 도시의 사진입니다. 도시에서 사는 장점은 매우 편리하다는 것입니다. 가게가 모두 가까이 모여있고 좁은 지역에서 할 일과 볼것들이 많습니다. 주요 단점은 일반적으로 매우 혼잡하다는 것입니다.

두번째 사진은 시골의 사진입니다. 시골 지역에서 사는 가장 큰 장점은 평화롭고 조용하다는 것입니다. 북적거림이 덜하기 때문에 일반적으로 삶에 스트레스가 덜할것 같습니다. 주요 단점으로는 고립 입니다. 당신이 무엇을 하려고 하든 먼거리를 이동해야 하는 불편함이 있습니다...

저는 시골에서 사는 것을 선호합니다. 왜냐하면 자연을 좋아하고 혼자있는것을 좋아하니까요. 큰 도시에서 사는 것은 꽤 정신없습니다.

SPA Exams

Exam1

Q1 Pronunciation

Describe the last time you enjoyed a night out with friends.

....

Do you prefer to go out on Fridays or Saturdays?

....

Q2 Listening Comprehension & Response Technique

Please listen carefully to the following paragraph about a Burger King restaurant owner and summarize it in your own words, giving as much information from the paragraph as possible. The paragraph can be repeated once.

Summary:
....
....
....

According to the paragraph, the owner redistributed his prize to his employees. What would you have done if you had won the same prize?

....

Have you ever had a similar experience where you won a nice prize?

....

Q3 Content & Use of Vocabulary

Not having a credit card can help you avoid buying unnecessary products. Is this effective?

....

What do you do to avoid impulsive shopping?

....

Listening files available online at www.mirinaeco.com

Q4 Grammar & Common Error

What would you do if you caught your son or daughter smoking or drinking?

....

Do you think underage drinking and smoking is a big problem in Korea?

....

Q5 Overall Fluency

Please explain what you see on this chart.

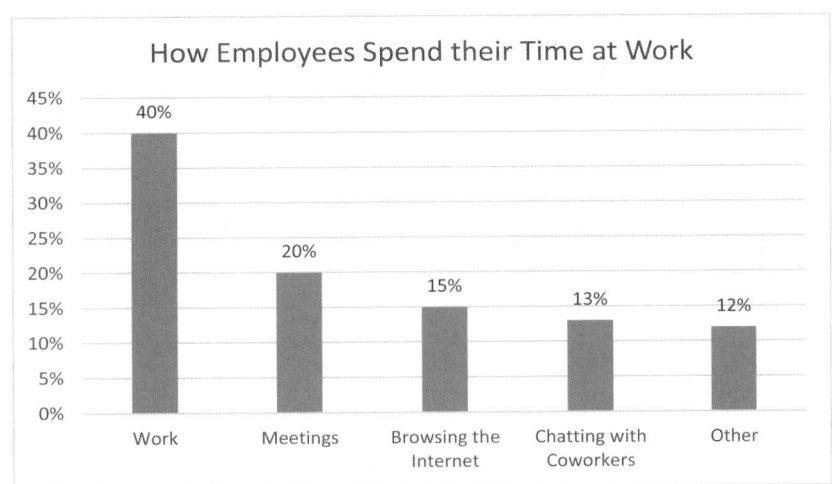

....

Exam2

Q1 Pronunciation

Who is your favorite musician? Why is he/she your favorite musician?

....

Do you prefer songs that came out recently or songs that came out a long time ago?

....

Q2 Listening Comprehension & Response Technique

Please listen carefully to the following paragraph about a precious item and summarize it in your own words, giving as much information from the paragraph as possible. The paragraph can be repeated once.

Summary:

....
....
....

According to the paragraph, the speaker damaged a very valuable item. What is one of the most valuable items that you damaged or lost?

....

What is one item that you could never replace?

....

Q3 Content & Use of Vocabulary

No matter how much money you have, you will always want more. How true is this statement?

....

If you had the freedom to do anything you wanted, what is the first thing that you would do?

....

Listening files available online at www.mirinaeco.com

Q4 Grammar & Common Error

Would you rather see a movie or a play?

....

Do you think people should be allowed to eat and drink during plays like with movie theatres?

....

Q5 Overall Fluency

The following graph shows the most used mobile apps in America. Please explain what you see.

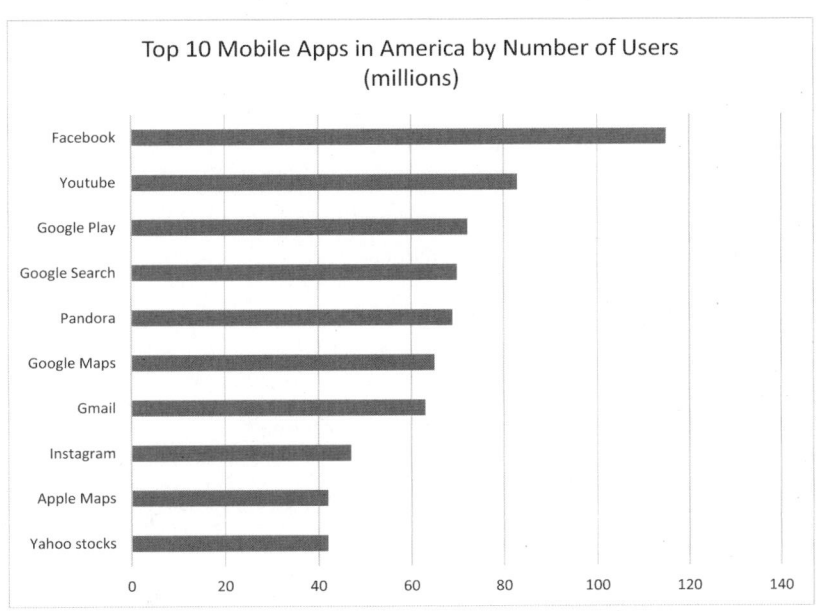

....

Exam3

Q1 Pronunciation

What was your favorite subject in school?

....

Which subject in school do you think is the least necessary?

....

Q2 Listening Comprehension & Response Technique

Please listen carefully to the following paragraph about memorizing names and summarize it in your own words, giving as much information from the paragraph as possible. The paragraph can be repeated once.

Summary:
....
....
....

According to the paragraph, the speaker is having difficulty memorizing names. What are some effective ways that you memorize people's names?

....

How would you feel if someone can't remember your name?

....

Q3 Content & Use of Vocabulary

Many customers use company websites to find useful information about its products. Please describe a company website that you think is well made. What's well made about this website?

....

Do you think all businesses nowadays should have a company website? Please explain why.

....

Listening files available online at www.mirinaeco.com

Q4 Grammar & Common Error

What are some rules parents should establish to ensure that their children behave well when at home?

....

Do you have any rules for yourself at home? If so, what are they? If not, what kind of rules do you think you need?

....

Q5 Overall Fluency

Please describe the following chart.

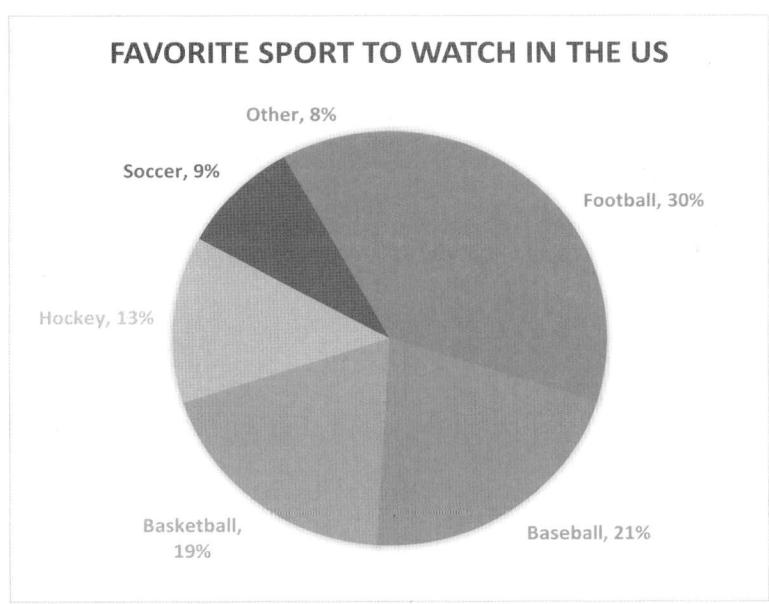

....

Exam4

Q1 Pronunciation

What is your favorite day of the week? Why?

....

Can you describe a memorable weekend you had with your family?

....

Q2 Listening Comprehension & Response Technique

Please listen carefully to the following paragraph about Bill Gates and summarize it in your own words, giving as much information from the paragraph as possible. The paragraph can be repeated once.

Summary:

....
....
....

According to the paragraph, Bill Gates is one of the wealthiest men on the planet. In your opinion, what are some advantages and disadvantages of being that wealthy?

....

If you were one of the wealthiest people on the planet, how would you use your position to positively influence the world?

....

Q3 Content & Use of Vocabulary

Many people consider a person's wealth and his or her ability to earn money as the most important aspect when considering a marriage partner. What is your opinion on this matter?

....

Is there anything that would immediately make you not want to marry someone?

....

Q4 Grammar & Common Error

What are some things you can do to avoid being late for work?

....

If you could change your starting time at work, what time would you change it to and why?

....

Q5 Overall Fluency

You are a shoe salesman and you are trying to sell me this shoe. Convince me why I should buy it.

....

Exam 5

Q1 Pronunciation

Describe your favorite dish?

....

If you ate nothing but your favorite dish for one week, how would you feel?

....

Q2 Listening Comprehension & Response Technique

Please listen carefully to the following paragraph about starting a business and summarize it in your own words, giving as much information from the paragraph as possible. The paragraph can be repeated once.

Summary:

....
....
....

According to the paragraph, starting a new business can be very challenging. Why do you think many people still want to start their own business?

....

Would you ever want to start your own business? If so, what kind of business? If not, please explain why.

....

Q3 Content & Use of Vocabulary

There are many factors to consider when buying a new house. What do you think are the most important things to consider?

....

Can you describe the house where you currently live?

....

Listening files available online at www.mirinaeco.com

Q4 Grammar & Common Error

What are the advantages and disadvantages of living in today's modern society?

....

If you could choose to live during any period in human history, when would you want to live?

....

Q5 Overall Fluency

Please compare the two pictures, explaining the similarities and differences.

....

Exam 6

Q1 Pronunciation

Describe a memorable holiday.

Which holiday is the most important to you?

Q2 Listening Comprehension & Response Technique

Please listen carefully to the following paragraph about stress and summarize it in your own words, giving as much information from the paragraph as possible. The paragraph can be repeated once.

Summary:

According to the paragraph, changing the way you think in stressful situations can help to produce better results. What are some effective ways you deal with stressful situations?

Can you recall a time when you had to overcome a stressful situation? What was it and how did you overcome it?

Q3 Content & Use of Vocabulary

People often consider buying lottery tickets as a waste of money. Others consider it a chance for fortune. Which do you agree with more?

Can you describe the last time you won a prize?

Q4 Grammar & Common Error
What are the advantages and disadvantages of being the only child in a family?

....

Would you want to be an only child?

....

Q5 Overall Fluency
Please tell us a story using this photo.

....

Exam 7

Q1 Pronunciation

What are some of your favorite topics when talking with your friends or coworkers?

....

What are some things you avoid talking about when at work?

....

Q2 Listening Comprehension & Response Technique

Please listen carefully to the following paragraph about convincing people to do tasks and summarize it in your own words, giving as much information from the paragraph as possible. The paragraph can be repeated once.

Summary:
....
....
....

According to the paragraph, people are more willing to agree to do an unwanted task if they are already used to doing smaller unwanted tasks. Do you agree with this statement?

....

What are some ways that you convince people to do unwanted tasks?

....

Q3 Content & Use of Vocabulary

Credit cards are a convenient way for people to pay for expensive items. What are some advantages and disadvantages of this?

....

Many people have more than one credit card. What do you think is a good amount of credit cards to have?

....

Listening files available online at www.mirinaeco.com

Q4 Grammar & Common Error

What is the best decision you've made this month?

....

Are there any decisions you wish you could change over the past month?

....

Q5 Overall Fluency

Please describe what is happening in the photo.

....

Exam8

Q1 Pronunciation

Do you prefer to wake up early or late? Give reasons.

....

Would you consider waking up at 7:30AM early or late?

....

Q2 Listening Comprehension & Response Technique

Please listen carefully to the following paragraph about air quality and summarize it in your own words, giving as much information from the paragraph as possible. The paragraph can be repeated once.

Summary:
....
....
....

According to the paragraph, there is a growing concern about poor air quality in Seoul. How concerned are you about the air quality where you live.

....

What are some things you can do to reduce the negative health effects of poor air?

....

Q3 Content & Use of Vocabulary

France and Hawaii are some popular destinations for couples. What are some important things to consider when choosing a romantic vacation?

....

Could you recommend a place to travel for a honeymoon couple?

....

Listening files available online at www.mirinaeco.com

Q4 Grammar & Common Error

Would you recommend buying a car in Korea? If so, why? If not, why not?

....

In Korea, there is a large important tax on foreign made cars. What is your opinion of this?

....

Q5 Overall Fluency

Compare the two locations pictured, describing the similarities and differences.

....

SPA Exams
Answer Key

Exam1

Q1 Pronunciation

Describe the last time you enjoyed a night out with friends.

최근에 친구들과 함께 재미있는 밤을 보냈던 경험에 대해 이야기 해주세요

Basic response	The last time I enjoyed a night out with friends was last Saturday. 마지막으로 친구들과 밤에 나가 놀았던 것은 지난 주 토요일 입니다.
Advanced response	The last time I enjoyed a night out with friends was last Saturday. I met up with my friends from high school and we went out to eat at a Korean barbeque joint. We ordered some pork ribs and had some beer mixed with soju as well. Once we had a good amount of drinks, we all decided to go singing at a noraebang. 마지막으로 친구들과 밤에 어울려 놀았던 것은 지난 토요일입니다. 고등학교 시절 친구들을 만나 코리안 바베큐 레스토랑에 가서 식사를 했습니다. 우리는 돼지갈비를 주문했고 소맥을 시켜서 마셨습니다. 술을 마시고 우리는 노래방에 가서 놀았습니다.

Possible follow up question:

Do you prefer going out on Fridays or Saturdays?

금요일과 토요일중 어느 요일에 친구를 만나는 것을 선호합니까?

I prefer to go out on Saturdays because I have all day to relax before going out. On Fridays, I'm usually very tired from work.

저는 토요일에 나가는 것을 선호합니다. 나가기 전에 하루종일 쉴수 있기 때문이죠. 금요일은 보통 업무 끝나고 나서 너무 피곤해요

Q2 Listening Comprehension & Response Technique

Please listen carefully to the following paragraph about a Burger King restaurant owner and summarize it in your own words, giving as much information from the paragraph as possible. The paragraph can be repeated once.

버거킹 점장에 관한 이야기를 주의깊게 듣고 문장에서 나오는 가능한 모든 정보를 당신의 말로 다시 요약해 주세요. 이야기는 반복해서 한번 다시 들을 수 있습니다.

Listening Passage:

An owner of a Burger King franchise recently gave his employees bonuses totaling over $120,000 after he received prizes for winning Burger King's 'Franchisee of the Year.' The owner, who received a new car as well as a Rolex watch, sold his prize items and immediately redistributed the money to his employees. The bonuses had a significant impact on the lives of the employees, even helping one of the employees pay for his mother's surgery.

어느 버거킹 프랜차이즈점의 한 점주는 '올해의 버거킹 프랜차이즈'에 우승한 이후 직원들에게 $120,000 보너스를 나누어 주었다. 점주는 새 차와 롤렉스 시계를 받았으나 상품을 팔아 즉시 직원들에게 나누어 준 것이다. 보너스는 직원들의 생계에 의미있는 영향을 주었고 한 직원 어머니의 수술비에도 도움이 되었다.

Summary:

This paragraph is about (Main) a Burger King owner who recently won a prize for having the best Burger King franchise. (D1) The prize was a brand new car as well as a Rolex which combined was valued at over $120,000. (D2) Rather than keeping the prize for himself, he sold his prizes and gave the money that he earned from selling to his employees. (D3) It really helped his employees out and even helped one of them pay for his mother's surgery. (Conclusion) Overall, this passage is a great example of a business owner who considers his employees an important aspect of his success.

(Main) 이 문장은 최근에 올해의 버거킹 프랜차이즈에 우승한 한 버거킹 점주의 이야기 이다.
(D1) 상품은 $120,000 이상 값어치의 롤렉스 시계와 새 차 였다.
(D2) 그는 상품을 갖는 것 대신 상품을 팔아 직원들에게 돈으로 나누어 주었다.
(D3) 그 돈은 직원들에게 많은 도움이 되었고 한 직원의 어머니 수술비로도 사용되었다.
(C) 자신의 성공을 직원에게 돌린 훌륭한 비즈니스 사업가의 모델에 관련된 이야기 인것 같다.

Exam1

Q2 Continued

According to the paragraph, the owner redistributed his prize to his employees. What would you have done if you had won the same prize?

위 문장에서 점주는 그의 상금을 직원들에게 모두 나누어 주었는데 만약에 당신이 똑같이 상품을 타게 되었다면 어떻게 하겠는가?

Basic response

If I had won the same prize, I would have kept the prize for myself. The reason is because as an owner, I also worked hard to get the prize.

만약에 내가 같은 상품을 탔다면 나는 내가 간직할 것입니다. 내가 점주로서 상품을 타기위해 역시 열심히 일했기 때문입니다.

Advanced response

If I had won the same prize, I'd probably have done the same thing except maybe keep the Rolex. After all, the employees did most of the work in running the franchise and serving the customers well. I think as an owner, you have to recognize your employees hard work and what that owner did for his employees is an excellent example of that.

만약에 내가 같은 상품을 탄다면, 아마도 똑같이 행동할 것 같다. 다만 롤렉스 시계만 간직할 것이다. 어쨌든 직원들이 프랜차이즈 운영에 많은 일을 했고 고객에게 서비스를 잘했기 때문에 내 생각에는 점주로서 직원들이 일을 열심히 했다는 것을 알아야 하고 점주가 직원들에게 상금을 나눠준것은 좋은 예이다.

Possible follow up question:

Have you ever had a similar experience where you won a nice prize?

위의 이야기와 똑같이 어딘가에서 상품을 타본 경험이 있습니까?

Yes, I once won 50,000 Won from a lotto ticket. I treated my friends to dinner with that money.

네. 로또 5만원에 당첨된 적이 있습니다. 그 돈으로 친구들에게 저녁을 사주었습니다.

Q3 Content & Use of Vocabulary

Not having a credit card can help you avoid buying unnecessary products. Is this effective?

신용카드를 갖고 다니지 않는 것이 충동구매를 피할 수 있다. 이 것이 효과적입니까?

Basic response	No, I don't think it is effective. If I have cash, then I can still buy things. 아니요. 효과적이지 않습니다. 만약에 현금이 있으면 현금으로도 충동구매를 할 수 있으니까요.
Advanced response	It can be effective as long as you don't have any other means of buying at that moment like cash or a debit card. If you do have a debit card or cash on hand , then not having a credit card probably won't deter you from buying something if you really want it. 현금이나 체크카드 같은 그 순간의 구매방법을 갖고 있지 않는 조건에서 효과적일 것 같습니다. 만약에 손에 당장 현금이나 체크카드가 있다면 신용카드가 없어도 당신이 진짜 원하게 될 경우에는 단념하지 않을 것 같습니다.

Possible follow up question:

What do you do to avoid impulsive shopping?

당신의 경우 충동구매 쇼핑을 어떻게 피합니까?

If I want to avoid impulsive shopping, I leave my wallet at home when I go out. I only bring a limited amount of cash with me.

만약에 충동구매를 피하고 싶으면, 내 지갑을 집에두고 밖에 나갈 것입니다. 밖에 나갈때는 정한 만큼의 금액만 가지고 나가는 것입니다.

Exam1

Q4 Grammar & Common Error

What would you do if you caught your son or daughter smoking or drinking?

만약에 당신의 아들이나 딸이 흡연이나 음주를 하다 걸렸으면 당신은 어떻게 할 것입니까?

Basic response	If I caught my son smoking or drinking, I might not say anything. However, my wife will probably kick him out of the house. 만약에 내 아들이 흡연이나 음주를 하다 잡혔으면 나는 아무말도 하지 않을 것 같다. 그러나 아마도 내 아내가 아들을 집에서 내 쫓을 것 같다.
Advanced response	If I caught my son or daughter drinking I don't think I would be upset unless I saw that they were drinking excessively. Most Koreans drink anyways so I think it's bound to happen. However, if I caught my child smoking, I'd be very upset because that is something that I made my children promise me to never do. It's very bad for your health and once a person starts smoking, it can become easy for them to get addicted. I want my children to live long, healthy lives so I'd be very against them smoking. 만약에 내 아들이나 딸의 음주장면을 발견했을 경우 너무 지나치게 마시지만 않았다면 화를 내지는 않을 것 같다. 대부분의 한국인은 음주를 하기 때문에 이것은 일어날 수 있는 범위라고 생각된다. 그러나 만약에 내 자식이 흡연을 하다 잡혔다면 나는 매우 화 낼 것이다. 왜냐하면 이것은 내 자식들에게 하지 말라고 약속한 부분이기 때문이다. 흡연은 건강에도 매우 안좋고 흡연을 시작하면 쉽게 중독이 될 수 있기 때문이다. 나는 내 자식들이 건강하게 오래 살기를 바라기 때문에 자식들의 흡연을 반대할 수 밖에 없다.

Possible follow up question:

Do you think underage drinking and smoking is a big problem in Korea?

한국에서 미성년자들이 음주를 하거나 흡연을 하는 것이 큰 문제입니까?

Yes, it's a big problem in Korea. There are many high school and middle school children that drink and smoke.

네. 한국에서 큰 문제입니다. 많은 중고생들이 음주를 하고 흡연을 하고 있습니다.

Q5 Overall Fluency

Please explain what you see on this chart.

차트를 보고 설명해 보시오

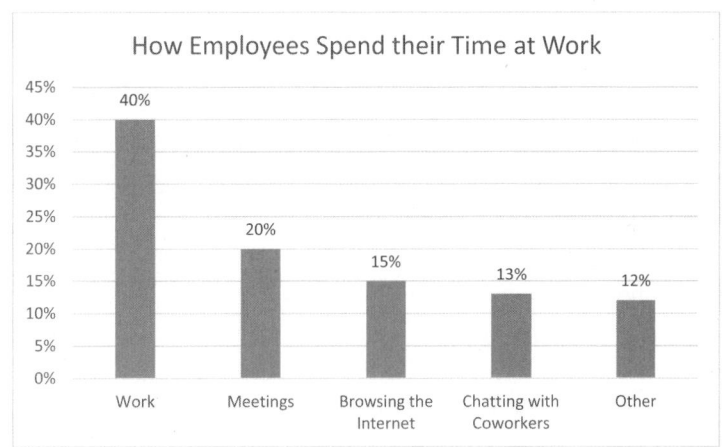

The graph depicts (Main) how employees spend their time at work. (D1) Forty percent of the time, people are actually doing work and the rest of the time they are doing something else. (D2) The most amount of time spent outside of work is meetings with 20 percent of the time going into that. (D3) Fifteen percent of the time is spent on the internet, thirteen percent of the time is spent chatting with coworkers, and twelve percent of the time is spent doing other things. (Analysis) Overall, it seems that even while at work, most people don't even spend half their time actually doing work.

(Main) 그래프는 직원들이 직장에서 어떻게 시간을 보내는지 보여 주고 있다.
(D1) 40퍼센트의 시간은 직원들이 일에 집중하여 시간을 보내고 나머지 시간은 다른 것에 시간을 소비하고 있다.
(D2) 업무외에 가장 큰 시간을 소비하는 것은 20%의 시간을 소비하는 미팅이다.
(D3) 15%의 시간을 소비하는 것은 인터넷이고, 13%의 시간을 소비하는 하는 것은 동료와의 채팅이다. 그리고 12%의 시간은 다른 것에 소비되고 있다.
(A) 전체적으로 봐서 대부분의 사람들은 업무의 집중시간이 업무시간의 반도 안되게 일을 하고 있는 것으로 보인다.

Exam2

Q1 Pronunciation

Who is your favorite musician? Why is he/she your favorite musician?

가장 좋아하는 뮤지션은 누구입니까? 그/그녀를 가장 좋아하는 이유는 무엇입니까?

Basic response

My favorite musician is Cho Yong Pil. He is a very famous Korean singer. The reason I like him is because he has a very nice voice and he sings about Korean culture.

제가 가장 좋아하는 뮤지션은 조용필입니다. 한국에서 매우 유명한 가수입니다. 그를 좋아하는 이유는 좋은 목소리와 한국 문화에 대해 노래를 불렀기 때문입니다.

Advanced response

My favorite musician is Yiruma. He's a famous Korean pianist. The reason why he's my favorite is because most of his songs are simple and easy to listen to. His music is great to listen to on rainy days or if you want to relax.

저는 이루마를 가장 좋아합니다. 그는 유명한 한국인 피아니스트입니다. 그를 좋아하는 이유는 그의 대부분의 노래는 단순하고 듣기 편하기 때문입니다. 특히 비오는 날이나 쉬고 싶을때 듣기에 매우 좋습니다.

Possible follow up question:

Do you prefer songs that came out recently or songs that came out a long time ago?

최신 음악을 좋아하시나요 아니면 오래된 음악을 좋아하시나요?

I prefer songs that came out a long time ago because if I listen to old songs, it reminds me of when I was younger.

저는 오래된 음악을 듣기 좋아합니다. 왜냐하면 옛날 음악을 들으면 내가 어렸을 때를 떠올리게 하니깐요.

Q2 Listening Comprehension & Response Technique

Please listen carefully to the following paragraph about a precious item and summarize it in your own words, giving as much information from the paragraph as possible. The paragraph can be repeated once.

소중한 물건에 관한 이야기를 주의깊게 듣고 문장에서 나오는 가능한 모든 정보를 당신의 말로 다시 요약해 주세요. 이야기는 반복해서 한번 다시 들을 수 있습니다.

Listening Passage:

The other night, I was drinking some coffee on my bed when I accidentally knocked the cup over and spilled coffee all over my wife's favorite blanket. I tried my best to get the stain out but it simply wouldn't come out. This blanket is very precious to my wife because it was passed down to her by her great grandmother. I'm worried that if my wife finds out, she'll be furious especially since she already told me several times not to eat or drink on our bed.

지난 밤에, 내 침대에서 커피를 마시고 있을때 실수로 컵을 떨어뜨려 아내가 가장 좋아하는 이불에 커피를 쏟았다. 얼룩을 지우기 위해 노력했으나 모든 얼룩을 지우기는 어려웠다. 이 이불은 내 아내에게 매우 특별한 이불이었다. 왜냐하면 아내의 증조할머니때부터 물려 받은 것이기 때문이다. 아내가 이것을 발견할까 걱정스러웠다. 아내는 매우 화를 낼 것이기 때문이다. 왜냐하면 매번 침대에서 음식을 먹거나 마시지 말라고 말해왔기 때문이다.

Summary:

The passage is about (Main) a man who accidentally spilled coffee all over his wife's favorite blanket. (D1) The speaker tried his best to remove the coffee stain but wasn't able to remove it. The reason why this blanket is significant is because (D2) it's a family heirloom passed down to his wife by her great grandmother. (D3) He's worried that his wife will find out about what happened and that she'll be furious because she specifically told him not to drink on the bed. (Conclusion) It seems to me that the speaker made a big mistake by not being careful with his wife's valuable possession.

(Main) 이 이야기는 실수로 아내의 소중한 이불에 커피를 쏟은 남자 이야기 이다.
(D1) 화자는 커피 얼룩을 지우려고 최선을 다했으나 얼룩을 지울수가 없었다.
(D2) 이불이 중요한 이유는 아내의 증조할머니때부터 물려받은 유물이기 때문이다.
(D3) 화자는 아내가 발견할 것에 대해 걱정하고 있다. 왜냐하면 아내가 이미 침대에서 음료를 마시지 말라고 특별히 말했었기 때문이다.
(C) 이내용은 화자가 아내의 소중한 물건에 대해 주의를 기울이지 않아 큰실수를 저지른 것으로 보인다.

Exam2

Q2 Continued

According to the paragraph, the speaker damaged a very valuable item. What is one of the most valuable items that you have damaged or lost?

위의 글에서 화자는 값 어치 있는 물건에 손상을 입혔다. 매우 비싼 물건을 손상시키거나 잃어 버렸던 물건은 무엇입니까?

Basic response

One of the most valuable items that I had damaged was my car. I accidentally hit a wall when I was trying to park and I damaged the back bumper. It cost me over 1 million won to fix.

내가 손상을 입힌 물건중 가장 값어치 있는 물건은 자동차 입니다. 주차하려고 할때 실수로 벽에 박은 적이 있습니다. 그래서 뒷 범퍼에 손상을 입었습니다. 수리하는데 1백만원 비용이 들었습니다.

Advanced response

I think one of the most valuable items that I've damaged was my old cell phone. To be honest, I actually threw it into the Han River because I was really upset at the time. I was waiting to meet my girlfriend there but after waiting for about an hour, she finally called me and said she wanted to break up with me. If I think about it now, I probably overreacted but at the time I wasn't thinking straight. Luckily, I was using that phone for almost two years so my contract was almost over. But still, it was a very expensive phone so I regret throwing it away.

아마도 가장 값어치 있는 물건에 손상을 입힌 것은 옛날 핸드폰인것 같아요. 사실, 핸드폰을 한강에 던져 버렸었어요. 왜냐하면 그때 너무 화가 났었거든요. 여자친구를 한강에서 한 시간정도 기다리고 있었는데 여자친구가 전화와서 헤어지자고 했어요. 지금 생각해보면 내 행동이 너무 심했던것 같은데 그 당시에는 바로 생각하지 못했어요. 다행히 그 핸드폰은 거의 2년을 써가고 있어서 계약기간이 끝나갈 쯤 이었어요. 그래도 그 핸드폰은 매우 비싼거여서 던진거에 대해서 후회 했어요.

Possible follow up question:

What is one item that you could never replace?

절대로 대체 불가능한 물건이 있습니까?

I don't think I could ever replace my wedding ring. That is why I never take it off my finger.

제 결혼반지는 절대 대체할 수 없을 것 같습니다. 그래서 손가락에서 절대 빼지 않아요.

Q3 Content & Use of Vocabulary

No matter how much money you have, you will always want more. How true is this statement?

당신이 돈을 얼마를 갖고 있던지 항상 더 많이 갖고 싶기를 원할 것입니다. 이 의견에 동의 하십니까?

Basic response	I think this statement is true because to me, having money means having the freedom to do whatever you want to do. Having more freedom is always a good thing. 저는 이 의견에 동의합니다. 돈은 자신이 원하는 것을 하는것에 대해서 자유를 주는 것입니다. 좀 더 많은 자유를 갖는 것은 항상 좋은것이라 생각합니다.
Advanced response	I would say this statement is generally false. After reaching a certain point of saving in which you have enough money to live comfortably for the rest of your life, I don't see the reason for having more money. Look at Warren Buffet for example. He has well over 50 billion dollars but he's planning to give the majority of it away to charity. I think if I were ever to have more than 10 million dollars, I wouldn't know how to spend it all in my lifetime. I'd rather spend my life enjoying the money rather than worrying about having more. 저는 이 의견에 동의하지 않는다고 말하고 싶습니다. 당신의 남은 여생을 충분히 편하게 보낼수 있는 만큼 돈을 갖고 있는 지점에 이르게 되면 그 이상 돈을 더 갖고 싶지 않을 거라고 생각이 듭니다. 워렌 버핏의 경우 500억 달러 이상이 있지만 그는 대부분을 자선단체에 기부 할 생각을 하고 있습니다. 내가 만약에 1천만달러 이상이 있으면 내 삶에 있어서 어떻게 소비할지 모를 것 같습니다. 더 많은 돈을 가지려고 걱정하는 것보다 이 돈으로 삶을 즐기며 사는 것을 선택할 것 같습니다.

Possible follow up question:

If you had the freedom to do anything that you wanted, what is the first thing that you would do?

만약에 당신이 원하는 모든 것을 할 수 있는 자유가 있다면, 처음에 무엇을 할 것 같습니까?

The first thing I would do is buy a mansion for my parents on Jeju Island. My parents really love Jeju Island and they have told me that they want to live there.

첫 번째로 부모님을 위해 제주도에 맨션을 하나 살 것입니다. 저의 부모님은 제주도를 너무 좋아하시고 거기에 정착하고 싶다고 말씀해 주셨거든요.

Q4 Grammar & Common Error

Would you rather see a movie or a play?

영화와 연극중 어느 것을 보기를 원합니까?

Basic response

I would rather see a play because when I see a play, it feels more real. Many stage performers interact with the fans to add even more realism to the play.

저는 연극을 보기를 원합니다. 연극을 보면 좀 더 실제 같거든요. 많은 무대에서 연극인들이 팬들과 상호작용을 해주어서 연극을 더욱 더 실감나게 만들어 주거든요.

Advanced response

While I enjoy watching plays, I think I'd rather see a movie simply because it's more convenient. If I go to the movie theater, I can dress casually and enjoy watching the movie in comfort. Another benefit of watching a movie over a play is the price. Plays usually cost a lot more than a movie ticket.

연극을 보며 즐기는 동안, 저는 차라리 간단히 영화를 볼 걸 하고 생각합니다. 왜냐하면 더 편리하니까요. 영화관에 가면 저는 캐쥬얼 하게 옷을 입고 갈수 있고 영화를 편안하게 즐길 수 있습니다. 영화를 보는 다른 장점은 가격입니다. 연극은 보통 영화 티켓보다 더 비쌉니다.

Possible follow up question:

Do you think people should be allowed to eat and drink during plays like with movie theatres?

영화관 처럼 연극보는 곳에서도 음식물 섭취를 허용해야 한다고 생각합니까?

No, I don't think so because it could distract the performers. Less distractions means that actors can concentrate on performing better.

아니요. 음식물 섭취는 배우들에게 방해를 줄 수 있습니다. 배우들이 방해를 덜 받아야 연극에 더 집중 할 수 있을 것 같습니다.

Q5 Overall Fluency

The following graph shows the most used mobile apps in America. Please explain what you see.

아래 그래프는 미국에서 가장 많이 사용되는 모바일 어플리케이션입니다. 그래프를 설명해보세요.

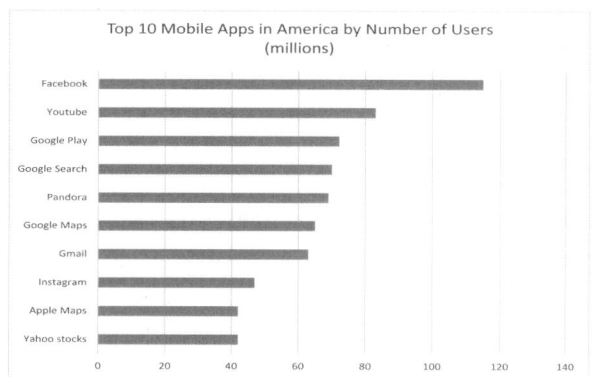

The graph shows (Main) the ten most popular mobile apps based on the number of users. According to the graph, (D1) the most popular mobile app in America is Facebook, which has 115 million users. (D2) The next most popular app is YouTube with 83 million users. (D3) Google Play is the third most popular, with 72.2 million people. (Analysis) It seems that Google has a strong hold of the American mobile app market, with Gmail, Google Maps, Google Search, Google Play, and Youtube all placing in the top 10.

(Main) 그래프는 사용자 수에 근거한 가장 인기있는 10대 모바일 앱 을 보여줍니다.
(D1) 그래프에 따르면 미국에서 가장 인기있는 모바일 앱은 1억1천5백만 사용자의 페이스북입니다.
(D2) 다음으로 가장 인기있는 앱은 8천3백만명 사용자의 유투브 입니다.
(D3) 미국에서 3번째로 인기있는 모바일 앱은 7천2백2만 사용자의 구글 플레이 입니다.
(A) 차트를 보니 구글의 Gmail, Google Maps, Google Search, Google Play 그리고 Youtube로 모두 탑 10에 들어가 미국 모바일 애플리케이션 시장에서 강력하게 자리잡고 있는것으로 보입니다.

Exam3

Q1 Pronunciation

What was your favorite subject in school?

학교다닐때 가장 좋아하던 과목은 무엇이었습니까?

Basic response	My favorite subject in school was science. The reason why I liked science was because we got to do interesting experiments like mixing chemicals and building model rockets. 학교 다닐때 가장 좋아하던 과목은 과학입니다. 과학을 좋아했던 이유는 화학약품을 섞고 로켓모델을 만들고 했던 경험이 흥미로웠기 때문입니다.
Advanced response	My favorite subject in school was world history. I especially enjoyed learning about ancient civilizations like the Roman Empire. To learn about all the extraordinary things that they accomplished such as their amazing infastructure and their conquest of Europe was truly fascinating. 학교 다닐때 가장 좋아했던 과목은 세계 역사입니다. 특히 로마제국같은 고대 문명에 대해 배우는 것이 즐거웠습니다. 로마제국이 설치한 수로라든지 유럽점령을 했던 업적은 정말로 대단했고 모든것이 매우 신기했습니다.

Possible follow up question:

Which subject in school do you think is the least necessary?

학교에서 중요도가 떨어지는 과목은 무엇이라 생각합니까?

I think physical education is the least necessary subject in school because students don't need to be in school to exercise.

제 생각에는 체육 과목이 중요도가 떨어지는 과목입니다. 왜냐하면 학생들은 학교에서 운동을 할 필요가 없기 때문입니다.

Q2 Listening Comprehension & Response Technique

Please listen carefully to the following paragraph about memorizing names and summarize it in your own words, giving as much information from the paragraph as possible. The paragraph can be repeated once.

이름 외우기에 관한 이야기를 주의깊게 듣고 문장에서 나오는 가능한 모든 정보를 당신의 말로 다시 요약해 주세요. 이야기는 반복해서 한번 다시 들을 수 있습니다.

Listening Passage:

Last week was my first week on the job. So far, I have really enjoyed working here. The work is easy, my boss is nice, and my coworkers are all very friendly. There is one problem though. My department has over 50 staff members and I'm having difficulty trying to memorize all of their names. They've all personally come and introduced themselves to me already so I'm afraid that if I ask for their names again, it might offend them. My wife suggested that I just ask my boss for their names.

지난 주는 직장에서 근무하는 첫 주 였다. 지금까지 이곳에서 일하는 것이 정말 즐거웠다. 업무는 쉬웠고, 직장상사도 좋았으며 직장동료들도 매우 친절했다. 그러나 한가지 문제가 있었다. 우리 부서는 50명 이상의 직원들이 있었고 그들의 이름을 모두 외우는데 어려움이 있었다. 그 동료들은 한 명씩 와서 자기 소개를 해주었기 때문에 나중에 다시 이름을 물어보는 거에 대해서 기분 나빠 할까봐 두려웠다. 나의 아내는 직장 상사에게 그들의 이름을 물어볼 것을 조언해주었다.

Summary:

The speaker just recently started a new job and although he enjoys working there, (Main) he is having difficulty remembering people's names. (D1) The reason is because he's working in a very large department with over 50 members. (D2) He doesn't want to ask them for their names again because he thinks that might offend them. (D3) His wife suggested that he should ask his boss for all of their names. (C) In summary, he needs a way to get his coworkers names without asking them directly.

(Main) 화자는 최근에 일을 시작하였고, 그곳에서 일 하는 것을 즐기고 있습니다. 화자는 사람늘의 이름을 외우는서에 대해서 힘들어 하고 있다.
(D1) 외냐하면 50명 이상의 큰 부서이기 때문이다.
(D2) 화자는 부서원들의 이름을 다시 물어보면 기분나빠 할 것을 두려워 해서 다시 물어보지 못하고 있다.
(D3) 화자의 아내는 화자에게 회사 상사에게 부서원들의 이름을 물어보라고 조언을 해주었다.
(C) 요약하면, 화자는 직장동료의 이름을 직접 물어보지 않고 알아내는 방법이 필요하다.

Exam3

Q2 Continued

According to the paragraph, the speaker is having difficulty memorizing names. What are some effective ways that you memorize people's names?

문장에 따르면 화자는 사람 이름을 외우는 거에 대해 어려움을 겪고 있습니다. 사람들 이름을 외우는 효과적인 방법이 있습니까?

Basic response	After I meet someone new, I keep repeating that person's name in my head. If I do this about 50 times, I usually remember that person's name. 새로운 사람을 만난 후에 나는 그 사람의 이름을 머리속에서 반복합니다. 약 50번정도 반복하면 보통 사람들 이름을 외우게 됩니다.
Advanced response	I think one of the best ways to memorize someone's name is to ask for that person's business card. If you receive that person's business card, you not only know the name but also what they do. I find that faces are easy to remember if you can remember what that person does so if you have his business card, then you can easily refer to that if you ever forget his name. If they don't have a business card, then I try to write down that person's name if I think it's important to remember him 제 생각에는 누군가의 이름을 외우는 가장 좋은 방법은 명함을 요청하는 것입니다. 상대방의 명함을 받으면 이름만 아는 것이 아니라 어떤 일을 하는지도 알수 있습니다. 그 사람이 무엇을 하는지 기억한다면 얼굴도 쉽게 기억할수 있습니다. 그래서 언제든지 그의 이름이 생각이 나지 않을때 참고할 수 있습니다. 만약에 상대방이 명함이 없고 상대방 이름을 기억해야 하는 중요한 자리이면 어딘가에 상대방의 이름을 적으려고 노력할 것입니다.

Possible follow up question:

How would you feel if someone can't remember your name?

만약에 상대방이 당신의 이름을 기억하지 못 한다면 어떠할 것 같습니까?

If we only met recently, then I don't mind. However, if we keep meeting and they keep forgetting my name, then I will probably feel upset.

만약에 최근에 만난 사람이었다면 신경쓰지 않을 것입니다. 그러나 계속 만났던 사람이고 계속해서 내 이름을 잊어버린다면 아마도 화가 날 것입니다.

Q3 Content & Use of Vocabulary

Many customers use company websites to find useful information about its products. Please describe a company website that you think is well made. What's well made about the website?

많은 소비자들이 제품 정보를 회사 웹사이트에서 찾아봅니다. 당신이 생각하기에 잘 만들어진 회사 웹사이트에 대해 설명해 보세요. 어떤점이 잘 만들어졌나요?

Basic response	I think Google is a well made company website because it has a simple user interface. There's hardly any advertisements and it's easy to find whatever information I want to find about the company. 제 생각에는 구글이 잘 만들어진 회사 웹사이트 인 것 같습니다. 왜냐하면 단순하게 사용자 인터페이스로 되어 있기 때문입니다. 광고가 거의 없고 어떤 정보이든지 내가 원하는 회사 정보를 쉽게 찾을 수 있습니다.
Advanced response	I think that Hyundai's global website is very well made because it caters to the user based on which country they are from. The website includes all the necessary information that an average consumer might be interested in such as what models are available, what their specifications are, where they can purchase the cars, as well as links to any corporate related questions a consumer may have. 제 생각에는 현대의 글로벌 웹사이트가 잘 만들어 진 것 같습니다. 왜냐하면 사용자가 어느 국가에서 왔는지에 따라 정보를 보여주고 어떤 모델들이 가능한지, 세부사항이 어떠한지 어디서 자동차를 구매할 수 있는지와 같은 보통 소비자가 흥미 가질만한 모든 정보를 포함하고 있기 때문입니다. 뿐만아니라 소비자가 가질 수 있는 기업 관련 질문돌도 연결되어 있습니다.

Possible follow up question:

Do you think all businesses nowadays should have a company website? Please explain why.

오늘 날 모든 비즈니스는 회사 웹사이트를 가지고 있어야 한다고 생각합니까? 왜 그렇게 생각합니까?

Yes, I think all businesses should have a company website these days because it is so easy to set up. It's an effective way to promote your business and make it look more professional.

네. 오늘날 모든 회사는 웹사이트를 가지고 있어야 한다고 생각합니다. 왜냐하면 설치하기 쉽고 당신의 비즈니스를 효과적으로 홍보할 수 있는 방법이며 회사가 좀 더 전문적으로 보여지기 때문입니다.

Q4 Grammar & Common Error

What are some rules parents should establish to ensure that their children behave well when at home?

가정에서 자녀들의 행동을 가르치기 위해 부모들이 만들어야 할 규칙은 무엇이 있을까요?

Basic response

Parents should make their children wake up and go to sleep on time. Also, they should make sure their children brush their teeth after eating.

부모들은 자녀들이 제시간에 일어나고 잠자리에 들도록 가르쳐야 합니다. 또한 자녀들이 식사후에 양치할 수 있도록 가르쳐야 합니다.

Advanced response

When I was growing up, my parents had some basic house rules that I thought were very effective. One was, no television until after I showed them my completed homework assignments. Another one was no food after 8 PM. Furthermore, she only served dinner at exactly 6:30. If we missed the time, we didn't get to eat. These rules were very effective at keeping me well behaved so I think these same rules would work on children nowadays too.

제가 자랄때 저희집에는 생각하기에 매우 실질적인 기본 규칙이 있었습니다. 하나는 숙제를 완벽히 끝내서 보여 줄 때까지 텔레비전 시청금지 였고, 다른 하나는 저녁 8시 이후에 음식 섭취 금지였습니다. 더 나아가 어머니는 정확히 6시30분에 저녁을 차려 주셨습니다. 만약에 식사시간을 놓치면 우리는 식사를 할수 가 없었습니다. 이러한 규칙은 제가 바른 행동을 간직 할 수 있도록 매우 효과적이었습니다. 그래서 저 역시 이러한 규칙을 저희 아이들에게도 적용시켜 교육하고 있습니다.

Possible follow up question:

Do you have any rules for yourself at home? If so, what are they? If not, what kind of rules do you think you need?

당신은 집에서 본인에 해당하는 규칙이 있습니까? 만약에 그렇다면 무엇이 있습니까? 없다면 어떠한 규칙이 필요한 것 같습니까?

No, I don't have any specific rules for myself but if I were to make one, it'd probably be to never eat anything past 9PM.

아니요. 제 자신을 위한 특별한 규칙은 만들지 않았습니다. 그러나 만약에 하나를 만든다면 9시 이후에 금식 규칙을 만들 것 같아요.

Q5 Overall Fluency

Please describe the following chart.

아래 차트를 묘사해 주세요.

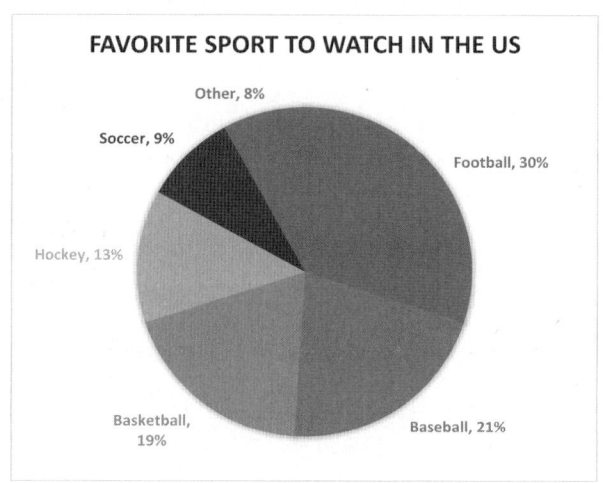

The chart represents (Main) America's favorite sports to watch. (D1) The most popular sport is football, with 30 percent of Americans selecting that as their favorite sport to watch. (D2) Baseball is the second most popular sport at 21 percent and is followed closely by (D3) basketball with 19 percent. (D4) Hockey's next at 13 percent and (D5) soccer rounds off the top 5 at 9 percent. (D6) 8 percent of the population prefers a sport not listed on this chart. (Analysis) It definitely seems like Americans love football.

(Main) 이 차트는 미국인의 스포츠 시청 선호도를 보여 주고 있다
(D1) 가장 인기있는 스포츠는 미식축구입니다. 미국인 시청 선호도 30%를 보여주고 있다.
(D2) 두번째로 인기있는 스포츠는 21%의 야구이고
(D3) 이에 근접한 차이의 선호하는 스포츠 시청은 19%의 농구이다.
(D4) 다음으로 13%의 하키이고
(D5) 축구가 9%로 Top 5로 마무리 된다.
(D6) 8%의 인기있는 선호 스포츠 종목은 차트에 나오지 않았디.
(Analysis) 표로 보아 미국인들은 미식추구를 매우 좋아하는 것으로 보인다.

Exam4

Q1 Pronunciation

What is your favorite day of the week? Why?

일주일중 가장 좋아하는 요일은 언제입니까? 이유는요?

Basic response

My favorite day of the week is Saturday. I like Saturdays because I get to relax at home with my family.

저는 토요일을 가장 좋아합니다. 토요일을 좋아하는 이유는 가족들과 집에서 쉴 수 있기 때문입니다.

Advanced response

My favorite day of the week is Friday because that's the last work day and I have the entire weekend to look forward to. Friday nights are usually the most fun too because that's when most people go out to party or spend time with friends.

제가 가장 좋아하는 요일은 금요일입니다. 왜냐하면 1주일 중 마지막 근무요일이고 1주일중 가장 기다리는 요일입니다. 금요일 밤은 보통 가장 재미있는 밤이기도 합니다. 왜냐하면 대부분의 사람들이 파티에 가거나 친구들과 시간을 보내기 때문입니다.

Possible follow up question:

Can you describe a memorable weekend you had with your family?

가족들과 잊지 못할 주말을 보내던 경험을 설명해 주세요.

Sure. Last Saturday was a memorable weekend because my family and I went to the zoo with my 5 year old son. It was the first time my son saw a tiger. He was really excited about it so it made my wife and me very happy.

지난 토요일은 잊지 못 할 주말이었습니다. 왜냐하면 5살 아들과 함께 동물원에 갔기 때문입니다. 우리 아들이 처음으로 호랑이를 보았습니다. 아들은 매우 신나했고 이것으로 저와 아내는 매우 기뻤습니다.

Q2 Listening Comprehension & Response Technique

Please listen carefully to the following paragraph about Bill Gates and summarize it in your own words, giving as much information from the paragraph as possible. The paragraph can be repeated once.

빌게이츠에 관한 이야기를 주의깊게 듣고 문장에서 나오는 가능한 모든 정보를 당신의 말로 다시 요약해 주세요. 이야기는 반복해서 한번 다시 들을 수 있습니다.

Listening Passage:

Bill Gates, co-founder of Microsoft and one of the wealthiest men on the planet, married Melinda French in 1994. Together, they established the largest private foundation in the world, the Bill & Melinda Gates Foundation. The foundation aims to enhance healthcare and to reduce extreme poverty worldwide. The Gates have personally donated a large portion of their substantial fortune to this cause. As of 2013, they have donated over 28 billion dollars.

빌게이츠 는 마이크로소프트의 공동 창업자이고 지구에서 가장 부유한 사람중의 한 명이다. 그는 Melinda French와 1994년에 결혼을 했다. 그들은 함께 세계에서 가장 큰 Bill & Melinda Gates 재단을 세웠다. 이재단은 건강관리 향상과 전세계의 극빈층을 줄이는 것을 목표로 하고 있다. 게이츠 부부는 그들의 상당한 부분의 재산을 개인적으로 이 재단에 기부하기도 하였다. 2013년부터 280억달러 이상을 기부하고 있다.

Summary:

The paragraph is about (Main) Bill and Melinda Gates' foundation. (D1) This foundation is the largest private foundation in the world. (D2) The foundation's mission is to enhance healthcare and reduce poverty worldwide. (D3) Bill and Melinda Gates have donated over 28 billion dollars to the foundation so far. (C) I think what the Gates are doing is a great example for other very wealthy people to follow.

(Main) 이 문장은 Bill & Melinda Gates 재단에 관한 이야기 이다.
(D1) 이 재단은 세계에서 제일 큰 개인 재단이다.
(D2) 설립자의 목표는 건강증진과 세계의 빈곤 퇴치이다.
(D3) Bill과 Malinda Gates 부부는 280억 달러를 재단에 기부하였다.
(C) 빌 게이츠 부부는 다른 재벌들이 따라야 할 좋은 모범적 행동을 하였다고 생각한다.

Exam4

Q2 Continued

According to the paragraph, Bill Gates is one of the wealthiest men on the planet. In your opinion, what are some advantages and disadvantages of being that wealthy?

위의 문장에 따르면, 빌게이츠는 세계에서 가장 부유한 사람중의 한명입니다. 당신이 그 만큼 부자가 된다면 장단점이 무엇이 있을까요?

Basic response

In my opinion, an advantage to being that wealthy is power. In Korea, if you are wealthy, you can control almost anything you want to. I don't think there are any disadvantages. Perhaps some people could say fame is a disadvantage if you're very wealthy but I actually want to be famous so it's not a disadvantage for me.

부유하게 되는것의 장점은 힘을 갖는 것입니다. 한국에서 돈이 많다면 당신이 원하는 거의 대부분의 것을 컨트롤 할 수 있습니다. 제 생각에는 단점은 없는 것 같습니다. 아마도 어떤 사람들은 유명해지는 것이 단점이라고 말 할 수 있습니다. 그러나 저는 또한 유명해지고 싶기 때문에 저에게는 단점이 아닙니다.

Advanced response

Being wealthy has a wealth of advantages. For starters, being wealthy allows you the freedom to do basically whatever you want to do. You could send your kids to the best schools money could buy for example. Not having to worry about my children's future is a huge advantage. As far as any disadvantages, perhaps being wealthy makes you a bigger target. People may try to coerce you into buying them nice things. Furthermore, you'll probably be expected to pay whenever you go out to eat.

부유해지는 것은 장점이 풍부합니다. 창업자에게는 경제적 여유가 당신이 원하는 일을 하는 것에 자유로움을 주게 됩니다. 자녀도 돈으로 갈 수 있는 최고의 학교에 보낼 수 있다. 아이를 키우는데 있어서 돈 걱정을 하지 않는 것이 커다란 장점입니다. 단점이 있다면 아마도 당신이 부유하다는 이유로 큰 타겟이 될 수 있을 것입니다. 사람들은 아마 당신에게 물건을 팔려고 노력할 것이고 더 나아가 외식을 하게 되면 언제나 사람들은 당신이 대신 지불할 것으로 기대할 것입니다.

Possible follow up question:

If you were one of the wealthiest people on the planet, how would you use your position to positively influence the world?

만약에 당신이 지구에서 가장 큰 부자중 한 사람이 된다면, 자신의 위치를 이용해 세계에 어떻게 긍정적인 영향을 끼칠 수 있을 것 같습니까?

If I were super wealthy, I would donate my money or even start my own foundation to help improve the living conditions in poor places like Africa. They especially need help getting clean water so I think I would focus on that first.

내가 만약에 매우 부자라면 기부를 시작할 것이고 내 소유의 재단도 만들어 아프리카의 낙후된 주거환경을 개선시킬 수 있도록 도와 줄 것입니다. 특히 그들은 깨끗한 물을 얻는 것이 중요하니 그 쪽으로 우선 초점을 맞추고 싶습니다.

Q3 Content & Use of Vocabulary

Many people consider a person's wealth and his or her ability to earn money as the most important aspect when considering a marriage partner. What is your opinion on this matter?

많은 사람들이 개인의 부유함을 고려하고 결혼상대를 고를때도 돈을 많이 버는지 중요하게 생각한다. 이 의견에 대해서 어떻게 생각하는가?

Basic response

While I think a person's wealth is somewhat important when choosing a marriage partner, it is not the most important. What's more important is how well you can understand each other's minds.

내 생각에는 결혼 상대를 고를 때 개인의 부유함을 보는 것은 중요하긴 하나 제일 중요한 것은 아니라 생각한다. 서로를 얼마나 이해하는지가 가장 중요한 점인 것 같다.

Advanced response

I think the mindset that wealth is the most important aspect when choosing a person's spouse was a lot more prevalent in the past than it is today. However, I do agree that there are still many people that consider this to be an important factor. I think what's more important is to find someone that is from a similar socio-economic background. I've seen many cases where two people from different financial backgrounds get married and get divorced later on.

배우자를 고를때 재산을 중요하게 보는 사고방식은 오늘날 보다 과거에 훨씬 널리 퍼져 있었던 것 같습니다. 그러나 많은 사람들이 이직도 배우지를 선택할때 재산을 본다는 것은 중요한 사실입니다. 제 생각에는 비슷한 경제 조건의 사람들이 만나는 것이 제일 중요한 것 같습니다. 주변에서도 다른 경제 조건의 커플들이 만나서 나중에는 결국 이혼하는 것을 많이 봐왔기 때문입니다.

Possible follow up question:

What is one thing that you want to avoid when choosing a spouse?

배우자 선택시 기피하게 되는 조건은 무엇입니까?

If my partner doesn't want to have any children, then I won't want to marry her.

만약에 아이를 갖고 싶어하지 않는 상대자라면 결혼하지 않을 것입니다.

Exam4

Q4 Grammar & Common Error

What are some things you can do to avoid being late for work?

지각하지 않기 위해 할 수 있는 것이 무엇이 있습니까?

Basic response	Some things you can do to avoid being late for work are things like going to sleep early, getting to work before rush hour, and skipping breakfast. 지각을 피하는 방법은 일찍자기, 러쉬아워 이전에 회사에 도착하기, 그리고 아침 식사 생략하는 방법들이 있습니다.
Advanced response	There's a lot of things you can do to avoid being late for work. The key is to prepare things in advance. For example, you can pick out what you want to wear the night before work and lay out your outfit on a chair. Rather than taking a shower in the morning, you can take one at night. Skipping breakfast isn't really healthy but if you are running really late and must skip it, perhaps you can have a box of nutrition bars ready just in case. 지각을 피하는 많은 방법들이 있습니다. 핵심은 미리 준비하는 것입니다. 예를들어 전날밤에 어떤 옷을 입고 갈 것인지 미리 준비해서 의자에 걸어놓는 것입니다. 아침에 샤워하기 보다는 전날 밤에 미리 할 수 도 있습니다. 아침 식사를 생략하는 것은 건강에 좋지는 않지만 정말 늦을 거 같으면 생략할 수 도 있습니다. 이럴 경우에는 에너지바를 준비해서 아침 식사 대용으로 먹어도 좋습니다.

Possible follow up question:

If you could change your starting time at work, what time would you change it to and why?

만약에 출근시간을 바꿀 수 있다면 몇 시가 좋습니까? 그리고 이유는요?

I would change my starting time to 11AM because then, I can avoid rush hour easily. Even if I had to finish later, I think it would be worth it.

저는 출근시간을 11AM으로 바꾸고 싶습니다. 왜냐하면 러쉬아워를 쉽게 피할 수 있기 때문입니다. 퇴근시간이 늦어져도 좋을 것 같습니다.

Q5 Overall Fluency

You are a shoe salesman and you are trying to sell me this shoe. Convince me why I should buy it.

당신은 신발 판매사원입니다. 아래의 신발을 판매하려고 합니다. 왜 사야 하는지 설득해보세요.

(Intro) If you're the type of person that likes to set fashionable trends, then look no further than this beautifully designed sneaker. (D1) The sleek, aerodynamic design not only makes you look sharp, it also (D2) ensures that you run faster than you've ever run before. (D3) The sturdy rubber bottom will allow you to walk over rough terrain in comfort. (D4) The entire shoe is covered with water resistant coating so you'll never have to worry about stepping into a puddle of water or being out in the rain. (C) Overall, a fantastic buy at the low price of only ten dollars.

(Intro) 당신이 만약에 패션 트렌드에 관심있는 사람이라면 이만큼 예쁘게 디자인된 신발은 더 없을 것입니다.
(D1) 매끄럽고, 공기역학 디자인은 당신을 샤프하게 보이게 할 뿐만 아니라
(D2) 당신이 더 빨리 달릴수 있게 도와 줄 것입니다.
(D3) 튼튼한 고무 밑창은 거친 지역에서도 편안하게 해 줄 것입니다.
(D4) 전체적으로 신발은 방수 코팅이 되어 있어서 물웅덩이나 빗속에서 걷는 것을 걱정하지 않아도 됩니다.
(C) 오직 10달러로 구매할 수 있는 낮은 가격으로 환상적인 구매입니다.

Exam5

Q1 Pronunciation

Describe your favorite dish?

제일 좋아하는 음식에 대해서 묘사해 보세요.

Basic response

My favorite dish is galbi jjim. It's my favorite dish because I grew up eating it and it is very delicious. I especially like my mom's galbi jjim because it is sweeter than other galbi jjims.

제가 가장 좋아하는 음식은 갈비찜입니다. 제가 자라면서 먹었던 음식이었고 무척 맛있엇기 때문입니다. 특히 어머니의 갈비찜을 좋아하는데 다른 어떤 갈비찜보다 달콤하기 때문입니다.

Advanced response

My favorite dish is called galbi jjim. It's one of the most popular dishes in Korea. It's a braised beef stew that's usually served with rice. The base sauce for the dish consists of soy sauce, sugar, minced garlic, and a sweet fruit such as a Korean pear or apple. The beef is first seared and then boiled in the sauce until it's so tender you can easily tear it off the bone. Other vegetables like carrots, potatoes, and onions are then added for even more flavor.

제가 가장 좋아하는 음식은 갈비찜입니다. 한국에서 가장 인기있는 음식중의 하나이기도 합니다. 갈비 찜 스튜 종류인데 항상 밥과 함께 제공됩니다. 음식의 기본 재료는 간장, 설탕, 다진 마늘 그리고 한국 배나 사과같은 달콤한 과일입니다. 소고기를 먼저 구운후에 소스가 부드러워 질때까지 함께 다시 끓이게 되면 고기가 뼈에서 쉽게 빠져 나오게 됩니다. 당근, 감자, 양파같은 다른 야채들을 첨가하면 더욱 풍미가 생깁니다.

Possible follow up question:

If you ate nothing but your favorite dish for one week, how would you feel?

아무것도 안 먹고 가장 좋아하는 음식만 1주일 먹는다면 어떠할 것 같습니까?

If I ate nothing but galbi jjim for one week, I would most likely feel great. I love eating galbi jjim so much I could probably eat it for a whole month.

제가 만약에 아무것도 안먹고 갈비찜만 1주일 먹는다면 저는 아마도 행복할 것 같습니다. 그만큼 갈비찜을 좋아하기 때문에 1달을 먹어도 문제 없을 것 같습니다.

Q2 Listening Comprehension & Response Technique

Please listen carefully to the following paragraph about starting a business and summarize it in your own words, giving as much information from the paragraph as possible. The paragraph can be repeated once.

창업에 관한 이야기를 주의깊게 듣고 문장에서 나오는 가능한 모든 정보를 당신의 말로 다시 요약해 주세요. 이야기는 반복해서 한번 다시 들을 수 있습니다.

Listening Passage:

Starting your own business can be a challenging endeavor. There are many standard challenges that new businesses face such as hiring the right people, building a brand, and having enough capital to cover initial costs. Among the biggest challenges is fatigue, as many business owners get stuck working much longer hours than their employees. This can often result in new business owners making poor decisions about their business. Although working hard is more or less required, finding a good pace and avoiding too much fatigue can produce better results.

자신의 비즈니스를 시작하는 것은 어려운 도전이 될 수 있다. 적당한 인원을 뽑고 브랜드를 만들고 초기비용을 만드는 것과 같이 새로운 비즈니스를 시작하기에는 많은 어려운점 들이 있다. 그 중에 가장 큰 어려움은 피로가 쌓이는 것이다. 왜냐하면 많은 비즈니스 사업가들은 그들의 근로자보다 더 오랜 시간동안 일에 매달려야 하기 때문이다. 이러한 것들은 때때로 비즈니스 사업가들이 그들의 비즈니스에 잘못된 선택을 할 수 있게 만든다. 열심히 일하는 것이 비록 더 혹은 덜 필요하더라도 자기만의 페이스를 찾아서 너무 큰 피로를 피하게 된다면 더 나은 결과를 창출해 낼 수 있다.

Summary:

This passage is about (Main) the challenges that business owners face when starting a new business. (D1) Some of the challenges include hiring the right people, building a brand, and having enough capital. (D2) According to the passage, fatigue is one of the biggest challenges because of the long hours. (D3) Because of fatigue, owners can make poor decisions. (C) The paragraphs suggests that new business owners could benefit from finding a good pace.

(Main) 이 이야기는 창업자가 새로운 비즈니스를 시작할때 직면할 수 있는 어려운 점을 말해주고 있다.
(D1) 적절한 사람을 구하는 것, 브랜드를 구축하는 것 그리고 자금을 충분히 가지고 있는 것들의 어려움들이 있다.
(D2) 이야기에 따르면 긴 업무 시간 때문에 쌓이는 피로도가 가장 큰 힘든 점이다
(D3) 피로도 때문에 창업자는 잘못 된 선택을 할 수 있다.
(C) 창업자는 자기만의 페이스를 찾아 일 할 것을 제안하고 있다.

Exam5

Q2 Continued

According to the paragraph, starting a new business can be very challenging. Why do you think many people still want to start their own business?

위의 이야기에서, 새로운 사업을 시작하는 것은 매우 어려울 수 있다고 하였습니다. 그런데 왜 많은 사람들이 그래도 자신의 비즈니스를 하기를 원하는 걸까요?

Basic response	The biggest reason why that I can think of is for the potential profits. The risk could be high but the return could be even higher. 가장 큰 이유는 잠재적 이윤 때문일 것입니다. 위험도가 높지만 돌아오는 결과가 더 좋기 때문입니다.
Advanced response	I think many people still want to start their own business because there is a lot of benefits as well. For example, if you are a business owner, you can choose your own working hours. In addition, you can keep all the profit for yourself. Moreover, you are the boss and do not need to follow orders. 제 생각에는 아직도 많은 사람들이 자신의 비즈니스를 하고자 하는 이유는 많은 이익이 있기 때문인 것 같습니다. 예를 들어 당신이 비즈니스 창업주이면 당신의 근무시간을 정할 수 있고 모든 이윤을 당신 자신이 가질 수 있으며 본인이 상사이기 때문에 다른 사람의 명령에 따르지 않아도 됩니다.

Possible follow up question:

Would you ever want to start your own business? If so, what kind of business? If not, please explain why.

창업을 생각해 본적이 있습니까? 만약에 그렇다면 어떤 비즈니스를 해보고 싶습니까? 생각해본적이 없다면 이유를 설명해 주세요.

No, I don't think I would want to start my own business. If I did, I think I would become really stressed because I'd worry about my profit. I'd rather have the reliability of getting a monthly salary at someone else's company.

저는 창업을 해보고 싶지 않습니다. 만약에 제가 창업을 했다면 정말 스트레스를 많이 받을 것 같아요. 왜냐하면 제 이익에 대해서 확신이 없어 걱정할 것 같아요. 다른사람의 회사에서 월급을 받으면서 생활하는게 더 나을 것 같습니다.

Q3 Content & Use of Vocabulary

There are many factors to consider when buying a new house. What do you think are the most important things to consider?

새 집을 구입할때 고려해야 할 많은 부분들이 있습니다. 어느 부분을 가장 중요하게 고려하십니까?

Basic response	I think the most important thing to consider when buying a new house is the location. Ideally, the house should be close to where I work. 집을 살때 가장 중요하게 고려해야 하는 부분은 위치인 것 같습니다. 이상적으로 말하면 집은 제 직장과 가까워야 합니다.
Advanced response	I think the most important thing to consider when buying a new house is the price. Before I start looking at different houses, I first figure out how much I can spend and only look at houses within my price range. Once I have a list of houses that fits my budget, I can then consider other factors like location and size. 집을 살때 가장 중요하게 고려해야 하는 것은 가격인 것 같습니다. 다른 집들을 먼저 보기전에 자신의 예산을 살펴보고 내 예산 범위내의 집들을 봐야 합니다. 내 예산에 맞는 집들의 리스트를 가졌으면 지역이나 크기 같은 다른 조건들을 보면 됩니다.

Possible follow up question:

Can you describe the house where you currently live?

현재 살고 있는 집에 대해서 설명해 주실 수 있습니까?

I live in a three bedroom apartment with my wife and two daughters. The main entrance goes into our living room. To the right of the living room is our kitchen and to the left are our bedrooms. The bathroom is located right next to our bedrooms.

저는 아내와 두 딸과 함께 방 3개짜리 아파트에서 살고 있습니다. 출입구로 들어가면 거실이 나옵니다. 거실 왼편은 부엌이고 왼쪽에는 우리 침실이 있습니다. 화장실은 우리 침실 오른쪽 옆에 있습니다.

Exam5

Q4 Grammar & Common Error

What are the advantages and disadvantages of living in today's modern society?

오늘 날 현대 사회에서 살아가는데 있어 장점과 단점은 무엇이 있습니까?

Basic response

An advantage is that I can communicate with friends and neighbors very easily. It's also easy to get information. A disadvantage is that there are too many people to compete with these days.

장점은 친구들 그리고 이웃들과 매우 쉽게 커뮤니케이션 할 수 있는 점입니다. 또한 정보도 쉽게 얻을 수 있습니다. 단점은 오늘날에 너무 많은 사람들이 있어 경쟁을 하며 살아야 한다는 것입니다.

Advanced response

The biggest advantage of living in today's society is information. Information is now readily available to anyone with a click of a button. If I'm curious about something, I can simply search on the internet and get an abundance of information instantly. A disadvantage of living in today's world is that the world is becoming an increasingly crowded place with much more competition than in the past.

오늘 날의 현대사회에서 사는 것의 가장 큰 장점은 정보인 것 같습니다. 정보는 이제 손쉽게 누구든지 버튼 하나만 누름으로서 이용 가능합니다. 만약에 무엇인가 궁금하다면 간단하게 인터넷에서 검색할 수 있고 즉시 풍부한 정보를 얻을 수 있습니다. 현대사회에서 사는 것에서의 단점은 과거에 비해 더욱 경쟁적으로 변했고 복잡한 장소로 변해 가고 있는 것입니다.

Possible follow up question:

If you could choose to live during any period in human history, when/where would you want to live?

인간 역사중에 돌아가고 싶은 시대가 있습니까? 언제로 돌아가서 살고 싶습니까?

If I could live during any time period, I think I would want to live during the Joseun Dynasty because I want to meet the legendary Korean hero, Yi Sun Shin. I want to thank him in person.

어느 시대로든 돌아갈 수 있다면 아마도 조선시대로 돌아가보고 싶습니다. 왜냐하면 성웅 이순신을 만나보고 싶기 때문입니다. 개인적으로 고맙다고 인사하고 싶습니다.

Q5 Overall Fluency

Please compare the two pictures, explaining the similarities and differences.

두 개의 사진을 비교해서 유사성과 다른점을 설명해 보세요.

(Similarity) In the first picture, it looks like they are gathered for a business meeting. In the second picture, it also looks like they are in a business meeting. (Difference) The difference is that in the first picture, it looks like everyone is involved in the conversation as opposed to the second picture where everyone seems to be listening to the man standing up. (Analysis) It looks like they are having more fun in the first picture.

(S) 첫번째 사진은 사람들이 함께 비즈니스 미팅을 하는 것처럼 보입니다. 두번째 사진도 역시 비즈니스 미팅을 하는 것처럼 보입니다.
(D) 두사진이 다른점은 첫 번째 사진은 모두가 참여해서 대화를 하는 것처럼 보이나 두 번째 사진에서는 모두 들 서 있는 남자의 이야기를 듣는 것 처럼 보입니다.
(A) 첫번째 사진의 사람들이 좀 더 즐거워 보입니다.

Q1 Pronunciation

Describe a memorable holiday.

잊지 못할 휴일에 대해서 묘사해 보세요.

Basic response

Last year's Chulseok was a memorable holiday for me because everyone in my family all gathered at my grandparents house. I got to meet my cousins, who I have not seen in over 5 years. It was good to catch up with them.

작년 추석이 잊지 못할 휴일이었습니다. 왜냐하면 모든 가족들이 조부모님집에 함께 모였기 때문입니다. 5년동안 만나지 못했던 사촌들도 만났습니다. 친척들과 함께 만난것이 즐거웠습니다.

Advanced response

A memorable holiday for me was Christmas when I was 7 years old. Back then, my father was working abroad so I didn't get to see him very often. However, on Christmas day, he surprised me by showing up with a bag full of presents. It was the first time I had seen him in over 6 months so I was delighted.

잊지 못할 휴일의 기억은 7살때의 크리스마스입니다. 그때 저희 아버지는 해외에서 일을 하고 있어서 자주 만나지 못했습니다. 그런데 크리스마스 날에 아버지가 가방에 선물을 가득 채워서 제 앞에 나타났습니다. 6개월만에 만나는 아버지라서 매우 기뻤습니다.

Possible follow up question:

Which holiday is the most important to you?

어떤 휴일이 당신에게 가장 중요합니까?

I think the most important holiday is New Years because it renews my resolve to succeed and achieve my goals.

저는 새해가 가장 중요한 휴일입니다. 왜냐하면 저의 성공과 목표를 당설하기 위한 결의를 다시 잡아 주기 때문입니다.

Q2 Listening Comprehension & Response Technique

Please listen carefully to the following paragraph about stress and summarize it in your own words, giving as much information from the paragraph as possible. The paragraph can be repeated once.

스트레스에 관한 이야기를 주의깊게 듣고 문장에서 나오는 가능한 모든 정보를 당신의 말로 다시 요약해 주세요. 이야기는 반복해서 한번 다시 들을 수 있습니다.

Listening Passage:

Stress is often associated with bad things. However, studies have shown that the physical effects of stress such as increased breathing, faster heart rate, and sweating, are identical to the body's response when doing something courageous. Further studies have found that people produce better results in stressful situations if they view it as a chance to show courage, rather than as something to fear. So the next time you find yourself in a stressful situation, think of it as a chance to be brave.

스트레스는 보통 나쁜 일들과 연관되어 있다. 그러나 연구에 의하면 숨이 가빠지고, 심장 박동수가 빨라지고 땀을 흘리는 것 같은 스트레스의 신체반응들은 무엇인가 용기 있을때 하는 행동의 반응과 똑같다고 한다. 또한 사람들은 스트레스를 받는 상황에서 더 나은 결과를 생산해 낸다는 것을 알게되었다. 사람들은 스트레스를 받을 때 무엇인가 두려워 하는 것 보다 용기를 보여줄 기회라고 여긴다. 그래서 만약에 당신이 스트레스 상황에 있다면 용감해 질 수 있는 기회라고 생각해라

Summary:

The paragraph is about (main) stress and how you can properly manage it. (D1) Although people can perceive it as a bad thing, the paragraph states that (D2) if you look at it as a chance to show courage, you can produce better results in stressful situations. (D3) The study found that the physical effects of stress matches that of courage. (C) In summary, if you think optimistically about a stressful situation, then it is going to help you better overcome the situation.

(main) 이것은 스트레스에 관한 이야기이며 당신이 스트레스를 어떻게 올바르게 관리할 수 있는지에 대해 이야기 하고 있다.
(D1) 사람들은 스트레스에 대한 인식이 나쁠 수는 있지만
(D2) 문장에서는 용기를 보여줄 기회를 보게 되면 스트레스 상황에서 더 나은 결과를 생산해 낼수 있다고 한다.
(D3) 연구에 의하면 스트레스 받을때의 신체변화가 용기있을때의 신체변화와 똑같다고 한다.
(C) 요약하면, 스트레스 상황을 낙관적으로 생각하면 상황을 더 좋게 극복하는데 도움이 된다.

Exam6

Q2 Continued

According to the paragraph, changing the way you think in stressful situations can help to produce better results. What are some effective ways you deal with stressful situations?

문장에 따르면, 생각을 바꾸면 스트레스 상황에서 더 나은 결과를 생산하는데 도움이된다고 한다. 당신이 스트레스 상황에 효과적으로 대응할 수 있는 방법은 무엇이 있습니까?

Basic response

I deal with stressful situations by talking to my wife. It really helps having someone who can listen to my problems and give me advice about what to do.

저는 스트레스 상황에서 아내와 이야기 하면서 대응해 나갑니다. 누군가 제 이야기를 듣고 무엇을 해야하는지 조언을 해준다면 정말 도움이 됩니다.

Advanced response

When I'm feeling stressed out, I often turn to music. If I need to calm down, I listen to some soothing songs to help me relax. If I need motivation, I listen to some of my favorite rock songs. In any case, I find that taking a little break and doing something that you enjoy can help change your perspective on the stressful situation.

스트레스를 받는 느낌이 날때, 저는 종종 음악을 틉니다. 차분해지고 싶을때 부드러운 음악을 들으면 긴장을 풀어주는데 도움이 됩니다. 무엇인가 동기부여가 필요할때는 제가 가장 좋아하는 락 음악을 듣습니다. 어떠한 경우에도 약간의 휴식시간을 갖고 제가 즐겨하는 것을 하면 스트레스 상황의 관점을 바꿀 수 있습니다.

Possible follow up question:

Can you recall a time when you had to overcome a stressful situation? What was it and how did you overcome it?

스트레스 상황을 극복했던 경험을 설명해주세요 어떤 스트레스였고 어떻게 극복했습니까?

Last year, I quit my job because it was too stressful. However, soon after, my wife told me she was pregnant. I was very stressed because I knew I had to find a good job soon. I asked my father for some advice and he helped me to find a better job by introducing me to a friend of his who owned a company. I was able to find a good job thanks to my father's help.

작년에, 저는 직장을 그만두었습니다. 너무 스트레스 받았기 때문입니다. 그러나 곧 아내가 임신했다고 알려주었습니다. 바로 좋은 직장을 찾아야 하기 때문에 매우 스트레스를 받았습니다. 아버지에게 조언을 요청하였고 회사를 운영하고 있는 아버지 친구 회사에 저를 소개 시켜주어 더 나은 직장을 찾는데 도움을 받았습니다. 좋은 직장을 찾을 수 있게 해준 아버지의 도움에 감사드립니다.

Q3 Content & Use of Vocabulary

People often consider buying lottery tickets as a waste of money. Others consider it a chance for fortune. Which do you agree with more?

사람들은 로또를 사는 것을 돈 낭비라고 생각하기도 하고 행운을 가져다 줄 기회라고 생각하기도 한다. 어느 쪽을 더 동의합니까?

Basic response

I think it is a waste of money. The chance to win money is so small that it is much better to just use that money to invest in something else like stocks.

제 생각에는 돈 낭비 인 것 같습니다. 로또에 당첨 될 확률이 매우 낮기때문이고 차라리 주식 같은 다른 곳에 투자하는게 더 나을 것 같습니다.

Advanced response

I look at playing the lottery as more of a chance for fortune. However, it's not something I expect to win. If I do win, great! But if I lose, it's not that much money and it's a nice way for me to have hope throughout the week.

저는 로또를 행운의 찬스를 갖는 방법으로 바라봅니다. 그러나 당첨되는 것을 기대하지는 않아요. 만약에 당첨되면 좋은 것이고 당첨되지 않아도 큰 돈이 아니기 때문에 단순히 1주일동안 희망을 가지며 지내는 것이 좋은 것 같아요.

Possible follow up question:

Can you describe the last time you won a prize?

마지막으로 상품을 탄 것에 대해 이야기 해 줄 수 있습니까?

The last time I won a prize was when I was playing go-stop with my friends. I ended up winning a few thousand wons. We don't play with that much money, it's mainly just for fun.

마지막으로 상품을 탄 것은 친구들과 고스톱을 쳤을 때입니다. 마지막에 이겨서 몇 천원을 땄습니다. 우리는 그렇게 큰 돈을 가지고 놀지는 않아요. 단지 재미로 합니다.

Exam6

Q4 Grammar & Common Error

What are the advantages and disadvantages of being the only child in a family?

외동아이의 장단점은 무엇입니까?

Basic response

The main advantage is that you don't have to share anything with a sibling. The main disadvantage is that you get less freedom from your parents.

장점은 형제자매와 어떠한 것도 나누어 가질 필요가 없는 것입니다. 단점은 부모로 부터 자유를 많이 얻지 못하는 점입니다.

Advanced response

The advantage of being the only child in a family is that you are the only one your parents have to support. That means that you can receive better things from your parents because they will have more resources to spend on you. Instead of growing up with generic clothes brands, maybe your parents can afford to buy you name brands like Nike or Calvin Klein. The disadvantage I think is that you will be a lot lonelier because you won't have a sibling to play with.

외동아이의 장첨은 부모로부터 원조를 받을 수 있는 유일한 자식인 것입니다. 이 뜻은 부모로 부터 더 나은 것을 받을 수 있다는 뜻입니다. 왜냐하면 많은 재산들이 당신을 위해 지출되어질 것이기 때문입니다. 성장할때 일반적인 브랜드의 옷 대신에 아마도 당신의 부모님은 나이키나 케빈클라인 같은 유명 브랜드 옷을 사줄 수 있었을 것입니다. 단점은 아마도 외로움일 것입니다. 같이 놀 형제 자매가 없기 때문입니다.

Possible follow up question:

Would you want to be an only child?

당신은 외동아이였으면 더 좋았을까요?

No, I wouldn't want to be an only child. I love having my brother and sister. Even though we have to share more things, we also help each other so instead of just having two parents to support me, I feel like I have my parents plus my siblings to depend on.

아니요. 저는 외동아이가 되고 싶지 않습니다. 형제 자매가 있는 것이 좋아요. 비록 우리는 서로 나누어 가지면서 자라왔지만 또한 서로 도와가면서 커 왔습니다. 부모님으로부터 도움을 받고 더불어 형제자매가 있어 추가로 의지가 됩니다.

Q5 Overall Fluency

Please tell us a story using this photo.

아래 사진을 보고 이야기를 만들어 보세요.

(M) The two men are on a business trip to Tokyo. (D1) Robert, the man on the right, is the CEO and (D2) Charles, the person on the left, is the top salesman at the company. (D3) Robert's company is called Kingsmen and they sell designer quality suits at affordable prices. (D4) They're talking about how their suits would sell very well in Japan, as most office workers there wear these types of suits. (C) They're hoping that this trip will earn them a lot of money.

(Main) 두 남자가 도쿄로 출장을 가고 있습니다.
(D1) 오른쪽에 있는 남자가 CEO 로버트입니다.
(D2) 왼쪽에 앉은 사람은 찰스인데 그는 회사에서 최고의 세일즈맨입니다.
(D3) 로버트이 회사는 킹스맨이라는 회사인데 합리적 가격의 디자이너 품질의 정장을 판매합니다.
(D4) 그들은 일본에서 그들의 정장이 잘 팔릴것이라고 이야기 합니다. 왜냐하면 일본 대부분의 사무직원들이 이러한 종류의 정장을 입으니깐요.
(C) 그들은 이 출장으로 많은 돈을 벌기를 기대합니다.

Exam7

Q1 Pronunciation

What are some of your favorite topics when talking with your friends or coworkers?

친구나 직장동료와 이야기 할때 가장 즐겨 말하는 주제는 무엇입니까?

Basic response

When I am with friends, I like to talk about our relationships. We are all married now so we always have interesting stories about our wives.

친구랑 있을때 저는 관계에 대해서 이야기 하는 것을 좋아합니다. 지금 우리는 모두 결혼했기 때문에 모두 항상 자기 아내에 관한 흥미있는 이야기를 합니다.

Advanced response

One of my favorite topics for discussion is sports. My friends and I are all sports fans so we meet whenever there is a big game. It's fun to talk about sports with them because they're all very passionate about their teams.

제가 가장 좋아하는 주제는 스포츠입니다. 친구들과 저는 모두 스포츠 팬입니다. 그래서 우리는 언제나 큰 게임이 있을때 만납니다. 친구들과 스포츠에 대해 이야기 하는것은 재미있습니다. 왜냐하면 우리들은 모두 자신이 응원하는 팀에 대해 열정적이기 때문입니다.

Possible follow up question:

What are some things you avoid talking about when at work?

일을 할때 언급하기 피하는 주제는 무엇입니까?

I avoid talking about personal things like my relationship when I'm at work. Occasionally, I might talk about personal stuff with some of my closest coworkers but that's usually outside of business hours.

저는 일할 때 제 사생활에 대해 이야기 하는 것을 피합니다. 가끔 가까운 직장동료에게 개인적인 이야기를 하기도 하지만 그럴때는 보통 업무이외 시간에 이야기를 합니다.

Q2 Listening Comprehension & Response Technique

Please listen carefully to the following paragraph about convincing people to do tasks and summarize it in your own words, giving as much information from the paragraph as possible. The paragraph can be repeated once.

사람 설득하기에 관한 이야기를 주의깊게 듣고 문장에서 나오는 가능한 모든 정보를 당신의 말로 다시 요약해 주세요. 이야기는 반복해서 한번 다시 들을 수 있습니다.

Listening Passage:

Researchers have found that people are more likely to agree to do an unwanted task for you if you ask them to do something easier first. For example, if a boss wants employees to stay late for work, they may initially start by asking their employees to stay just a few extra minutes. Once employees get used to the idea of working after hours, it becomes easier for the boss to ask them to stay much later than what they would usually tolerate.

연구에 따르면 사람들은 보통 쉬운 일을 먼저 부탁하면 나중에 하기 싫은 일도 해 줄 가능성이 크다고 합니다. 예를들어, 어떤 직장상사가 직원들이 늦게까지 남아 일하는 것을 원한다면 먼저 직원들에게 퇴근시간 이후 몇 분만 더 있어달라고 요청을 하면 직원들은 좀 더 남아 있는 것이 익숙해지고 이것은 나중에 직장상사가 훨씬 오래 있어달라고 해도 나중에는 그것을 그냥 받아 들인다는 것이다.

Summary:

(Main) This passage was about how bosses can gradually convince employees to do things they normally wouldn't do by getting them used to doing easier things first. (D1) Once employees get used to doing small favors for their boss, it becomes easier for bosses to ask them to do more unwanted things. (D2) For example, a boss may at first ask an employee to stay just a little bit late. (D3) Once that employee gets used to working a little bit late, they get them to stay even later. (C) I think the overall message is that small favors gradually lead to bigger favors.

(Main) 이 이야기는 직장상사기 직원들이 평소에 하지 않는 일을 처음에 쉽게 적응하게 하여 이렇게 점차적으로 받아 들일 수 있게 하는지 설명하는 내용이다.
(D1) 상사에게 작은 호의를 베푸는 것이 적응이 되면 이것은 상사가 직원들이 원하지 않는 일 을 시켜도 쉽게 받아 들여진다.
(D2) 예를 들면, 상사가 처음에는 직원들에게 조금만 늦게 퇴근하라 한다.
(D3) 그러나 직원들이 조금 늦게 가는것이 적응이 되면 나중에 더 늦게 가는 것도 받아들이게 된다.
(C) 제 생각에 이 이야기는 작은 호의가 큰 호의를 이끌어 낸다는 것을 알려주는 것 같다.

Q2 Continued

According to the paragraph, people are more willing to agree to do an unwanted task if they are already used to doing smaller unwanted tasks. Do you agree with this statement?

문장에 따르면 사람들은 이미 작은 부탁에 익숙해지면 기꺼이 원하지 않던 일을 들어준다고 한다. 이러한 상태에 대해서 동의 하십니까?

Basic response

I think I disagree with this statement. I think that if you keep asking people for small favors, they will eventually stop doing any favors for you.

이런 상태에 대해서 동의하지 않습니다. 만약에 계속 작은 부탁을 요청하면 상대방은 나중에 끝내 어떤 부탁도 들어주지 않을 겁입니다.

Advanced response

I think this statement is true, especially in Korea. In my office, everyone stays very late for work. It wasn't like this when I first started working there though. I think over time, the boss has asked us to stay late a little by little and now it is completely normal to stay late and no one seems to notice because everyone is doing it.

제 생각에는 이러한 상태는 사실인것 같습니다. 특히 한국에서는요. 제가 근무하는 회사에서도 모두들 매우 늦게까지 일을 합니다. 사실 맨 처음 제가 일을 시작할때는 이렇지는 않았습니다. 시간이 지나면서 상사가 조금만 더 남아서 일을 해달라고 요청을 했었고 이제는 모두들 늦게까지 일하는게 보통이 되었고 아무도 이상하게 생각하지 않습니다. 왜냐하면 모두들 그렇게 행동하니까요.

Possible follow up question:

What are some ways that you convince people to do unwanted tasks?

사람들이 원하지 않는 일을 설득 시킬때 사용할 수 있는 방법이 있나요?

Sometimes, if I want someone to do something I know they won't want to do, I actually ask them to do something even more difficult or unwanted. For example, if I want my daughter to eat two pieces of carrot, I'll actually ask her to eat 4 pieces. She'll immediately say no and I'll say okay, fine, how about two? Normally, she thinks that I'm compromising so she'll eat the two pieces of carrot that I originally wanted her to eat.

때때로 상대방이 원하지 않는 것을 내가 시켜야 할때는 나는 더 어려운 부탁을 처음에 물어봅니다. 예를들어 내 딸에게 당근 2조각을 먹게 하려면, 저는 먼저 4조각을 먹으라고 이야기 합니다. 딸이 바로 싫다고 이야기 하면 "알았어 좋아 그럼 2개는 어때?"하고 물어봅니다. 보통 딸은 내가 타협을 했다고 생각하지만 사실은 내가 원하는 만큼 그녀에게 당근을 먹이는 셈이 됩니다.

Q3 Content & Use of Vocabulary

Credit cards are a convenient way for people to pay for expensive items. What are some of their advantages and disadvantages?

신용카드는 비싼 물건을 지불하는데 편리한 방법입니다. 신용카드의 장점과 단점은 무엇이 있을까요?

Basic response

An advantage is that you don't have to pay for the expensive item all at once. A disadvantage is that some people can't control their spending with a credit card.

신용카드의 장점은 비싼 물건을 구매함에 있어서 한 번에 지불할 필요가 없는 것입니다. 단점은 어떤 사람들은 신용카드 사용을 컨트롤 하기 어렵다는 것입니다.

Advanced response

I'd say the biggest advantage of paying for something with a credit card is the flexible payment options. I can choose to pay for it all at once without incurring interest or I can choose to pay in smaller increments for a small fee. In addition, credit cards often come with bonuses like 5% cash back or airline mileage. The disadvantage to using credit cards is that if you are late on a payment, you get a lot of penalties that end up costing you a ton of money.

신용카드의 가장 큰 장점은 유연한 지불조건 방식입니다. 이자를 발생 시키지 않고 일시불로 지불하는 방법 혹은 약간의 수수료를 부담하여 할부로 지불하는 방법등을 선택할 수 있습니다. 게다가 신용카드는 항공사 마일리지 라든가 5% 캐쉬백 같은 보너스를 제공하기도 합니다. 신용카드 사용의 단점은 지불해야 하는 날짜에 늦게 된다면 돈을 더 많이 지불해야 하는 페널티를 받을 수 있다는 것입니다.

Possible follow up question:

Many people have more than one credit card. What do you think is a good amount of credit cards to have?

많은 사람들이 한 장 이상의 신용카드를 가지고 있습니다. 몇 장의 신용카드를 갖고 있는 것이 좋은 것 같습니까?

I think having two credit cards is ideal because some credit cards don't work in certain places. I like to use my American Express card whenever I can because it comes with a lot of benefits but if some place doesn't accept my American Express card, I will use my Visa card instead.

제 생각에는 두 장의 신용카드를 갖고 있는 것이 이상적인 것 같습니다. 왜냐하면 때때로 어떤 특정 신용카드는 특정 장소에서 사용이 안될 수도 있기 때문입니다. 저는 아메리칸 익스프레스 카드를 사용하는 것을 좋아합니다. 왜냐하면 많은 혜택을 제공하기 때문입니다. 그러나 어떤 장소에서는 사용이 되지 않기 때문에 그럴 때는 제 비자카드를 사용합니다.

Q4 Grammar & Common Error

What is the best decision you've made this month?

이번 달에 당신이 한 일 중 가장 최고의 선택은 무엇이었습니까?

Basic response	The best decision I made this month was buying my girlfriend candy on White Day. One of my friends didn't buy his girlfriend candy on White Day and his girlfriend ended up complaining to him the entire month. 이번달에 제가 한 가장 최고의 선택은 화이트데이때 여자친구에게 사탕을 사 준 것입니다. 제 친구중의 한 명은 화이트데이날에 여자친구에게 사탕을 사주지 않아 한 달동안 계속 원망 받았다고 합니다.
Advanced response	The best decision I made this month was climbing Mt. Bukhansan. I was able to enjoy the fresh air and see the beautiful spring scenery. All the trees and flowers were starting to blossom so it was a great time to go hiking. If you haven't gone hiking yet, I'd highly recommend going now before the weather starts to get too hot. 이번 달에 한 최고의 선택은 북한산 등반이었습니다. 신선한 공기를 즐길 수 있었고 아름다운 봄 경치를 구경할 수 있었습니다. 모든 나무와 꽃들이 봉우리를 맺기 시작하였기 때문에 하이킹 하기 매우 좋은 시간 이었습니다. 아직 하이킹을 가보지 못했다면 날씨가 더워지기 전에 꼭 가보는 것을 강력 추천합니다.

Possible follow up question:

Are there any decisions you wish you could change over the past month?

지난 달 결정한 것을 번복한 적이 있습니까?

Yes, I wish I had spent more time studying English. I made a goal of studying at least 30 minutes every night but I ended up only doing it a few times.

네, 영어공부하는데 많은 시간을 보내려고 결심했었습니다. 매일밤에 최소 30분이상 공부하는 목표를 세웠으나 몇 번 하고 그만두었습니다.

Q5 Overall Fluency

Please describe what is happening in the photo.

사진에서 어떤일이 일어나고 있는지 묘사해 보세요.

(Main) This picture is showing elderly men and women taking a break by resting their feet in a public foot bath. (D1) Most of the people are sitting down but there is one man who seems to be walking around. (D2) It looks like the weather is somewhat cold because most of them are wearing long sleeve shirts or a jacket. (D3) The bottom of the fountain seems to be covered with smooth rocks to perhaps massage your feet. (A) Overall, it looks fairly relaxing and I'd love to try it some day.

(Main) 이 사진은 노인과 여성들이 공중 족욕탕에서 발 을 담그며 휴식을 취하고 있는 것을 보여주고 있습니다.
(D1) 대부분의 사람들이 앉아 있으나 한 남자만이 걸어다니는 것으로 보입니다.
(D2) 날씨는 조금 추워 보입니다. 왜냐하면 대부분의 사람들이 긴 팔을 입거나 자켓을 입었기 때문입니다.
(D3) 물 바닥은 아마도 발 마사지를 위한 매끄러운 돌로 깔려있습니다
(A)전체적으로 꽤 편안해 보이며 언젠가 저도 해 보고 싶습니다.

Exam8

Q1 Pronunciation

Do you prefer to wake up early or late? Give reasons.

아침에 일찍 일어나는것을 좋아합니까? 늦게 일어나는 것을 좋아합니까? 이유는요?

Basic response

I prefer to wake up early because I have more time to prepare for the day ahead.

저는 일찍 일어나는 것을 선호합니다. 왜냐하면 아침에 미리 준비할 시간이 많이 생기기 때문입니다.

Advanced response

I prefer to wake up late. To be honest, I'm more of a night owl so waking up early is a lot harder for me, especially if I sleep late. I feel a lot more productive during the night time though so I will usually sleep and wake up very late.

저는 늦게 일어나는 것을 선호합니다. 저는 사실 밤에 활동하는 올빼미족입니다. 특히 밤 새도록 있었거나 늦게 잠이들면 아침에 일찍 일어나는게 너무 힘듭니다. 밤에 일하는게 더 생산적이기 때문에 보통 자면 아침에 늦게 일어납니다.

Possible follow up question:

Would you consider waking up at 7:30AM early or late?

7:30AM에 일어나는 것이 이른 시간입니까 ? 늦은 시간입니까?

I would consider that early. I usually wake up at around 8:00AM to get to work on time but if it's the weekend, I usually sleep in until 9:00.

저는 이른시간이라고 생각합니다. 보통 8시 쯤에 일어나서 회사에 갑니다. 그러나 주말에는 보통 9시까지 잡니다.

Q2 Listening Comprehension & Response Technique

Please listen carefully to the following paragraph about air quality and summarize it in your own words, giving as much information from the paragraph as possible. The paragraph can be repeated once.

공기의 질에 관한 이야기를 주의깊게 듣고 문장에서 나오는 가능한 모든 정보를 당신의 말로 다시 요약해 주세요. 이야기는 반복해서 한번 다시 들을 수 있습니다.

Listening Passage:

There has been a growing concern about the poor air quality in Seoul recently. The city government issues a fine dust particle warning when the amount of fine dust in the air reaches levels that are considered unhealthy. Last year, the government issued the warning a record 11 times. Many residents resort to wearing protective masks during these days. Some residents even go as far as to not go outside. Officials recommend limiting outdoor activities on such days.

최근들어 서울에서 나쁜 공기에 관한 관심이 증가하고 있다. 서울시는 공기중 미세먼지의 양이 해로운 수준에 도달할 경우 경보를 보내기로 하였다. 작년에는 이러한 경보를 11차례 내보내는 기록을 세웠다. 요즘에는 많은 시민들이 미세먼지 방지 마스크를 사용하고 있다. 심지어 어떤 시민들은 밖에 멀리 나가지 않기도 한다. 당국은 이러한 날에 야외활동을 제한하는 것이 좋다고 한다.

Summary:

(Main) This passage is about the recent poor air quality in Seoul. (D1) The city officials send out a public advisory whenever the amount of fine dust particles in the air exceeds an unhealthy amount. (D2) According to the paragraph, the city issued this warning 11 times last year which was the most they've ever issued. (D3) The officials recommend limiting the amount of outdoor activities during these days. (C)I think it's a good idea to wear a mask on these days.

(Main) 이 문장은 최근 서울의 나쁜 공기에 대한 이야기 이다.
(D1) 서울시는 미세먼지의 양이 해로운 수준에 도달하면 경보를 내보낸다.
(D2) 문장에 따르면 작년에 경보 안내를 가장 많은 11차례나 내보냈다고 한다.
(D3) 서울시는 이러한 날에 야외활동을 제한하는 것이 좋다고 하였다.
(C) 내 생각에는 이런 날에 마스크를 쓰는 것이 좋은 것 같습니다.

Exam8

Q2 Continued

According to the paragraph, there is a growing concern about poor air quality in Seoul. How concerned are you about the air quality where you live.

문장에 따르면 나쁜 공기에 대한 관심이 증가하고 있다고 한다. 당신이 지금 살고 있는 곳의 공기에 대해 얼마나 관심이 있는가?

Basic response

I am very concerned about the air quality. I live in Ulsan and there are a lot of factories there. The factories produce bad air so the air in the city can get very bad sometimes.

저는 공기 질에 대해 매우 관심을 갖고 있습니다. 저는 울산에 살고 있고 거기에는 많은 공장들이 있습니다. 공장들이 나쁜 공기를 내뿜고 있기 때문에 도시 공기가 가끔 매우 나쁘기도 합니다.

Advanced response

I'm a little concerned about the recent decline in air quality but I feel that the overall air quality where I live is still fairly decent because of all the forests and mountains surrounding my area. If I were living in a major city however, I think I'd be much more concerned about the air quality.

저는 최근 공기가 나빠지는 것에 대해 조금 신경은 쓰이지만 크게 걱정은 없습니다. 왜냐하면 제가 사는 지역의 공기는 전체적으로 아직 꽤 좋기 때문입니다. 우리 동네는 산과 숲들이 둘러쌓여 있기 때문입니다. 만약에 제가 주요 도시에서 살았다면 공기의 질에 대해서 더욱 관심을 가졌을 것입니다.

Possible follow up question:

What are some things your city can do to improve the air quality?

당신의 도시가 공기의 질을 향상시키기위해 무엇을 할 수 있습니까?

I think the easiest way my city can improve the air quality is to plant more trees along the roads. Another thing my city could do is to create more bicycle lanes so that more people will ride their bikes rather than a car.

제 생각에 우리 도시가 공기의 질을 향상 시키는 쉬운 방법은 길가에 나무를 좀 더 심는 것입니다.
우리 도시가 할 수 있는 다른 것들은 자전거 도로를 만들어 많은 사람들이 자동차 대신에 자전거를 타고 다니게 하는 것입니다.

Q3 Content & Use of Vocabulary

France and Hawaii are some popular destinations for couples. What are some important things to consider when choosing a romantic vacation?

프랑스와 하와이는 커플들의 여행지로 유명합니다. 로맨틱한 휴가를 선택함에 있어서 중요하게 고려해야 하는 부분은 무엇입니까?

Basic response

I think finding a nice hotel is very important for a romantic vacation. Another important thing is finding a romantic restaurant in the area you plan to visit.

제 생각에는 로맨틱한 휴가를 위해 좋은 호텔을 선택하는 것이 매우 중요하다고 생각합니다. 다른 중요한 점은 방문하기로 한 지역의 로맨틱한 식당을 찾는 것도 중요합니다.

Advanced response

For me, having beautiful scenery is essential for romance so I think planning a vacation to romantic areas like Paris or Maui is important. Finding a luxurious resort with a romantic ambiance is also helpful for a romantic atmosphere. Lastly, you must have privacy so reserving a room that is secluded will help.

저는 아름다운 경치를 갖는 것이 로맨스의 필수라고 생각합니다. 파리나 마우이 같이 로맨틱한 장소로 휴가계획을 세우는 것이 중요합니다. 로맨틱한 장식의 럭셔리한 리조트를 찾는 것 또한 분위기를 내는데 도움이 됩니다. 마지막으로 사생활을 신경써야 하기 때문에 외딴 곳의 방으로 예약하는 것이 도움이 됩니다.

Possible follow up question:

Could you recommend a place to travel for a honeymoon couple?

허니문 커플들을 위한 장소를 추천해줄 수 있습니까?

Sure, I would recommend honeymooners to go to Guam. It's not as far or as expensive as Hawaii but you still have the luxury of beautiful beaches and nice hotels.

물론입니다. 저는 괌으로 가는 것을 추천합니다. 하와이같이 비싸고 멀지도 않으면서 고급스럽고 아름다운 바닷가와 좋은 호텔들을 가지고 있습니다.

Exam8

Q4 Grammar & Common Error

Would you recommend buying a car in Korea? If so, why? If not, why not?

한국에서 자동차를 사는 것을 추천하겠습니까? 이유는요? 그렇지 않다면 이유는요?

Basic response

No, I would not recommend buying a car in Korea. Driving in Korea is too stressful with all the cars on the roads. In addition, the public transportation in Korea is excellent so there is no need to own a car.

저는 한국에서 자동차를 사는것을 추천하지 않습니다. 도로위의 많은 차들과 함께 운전하는 것은 너무 큰 스트레스입니다. 게다가 한국의 대중교통은 매우 훌륭하기 때문에 자가용이 필요없습니다.

Advanced response

I think it depends on what your needs are but if you asked me if it's necessary to buy a car in Korea, I'd say no because there are a lot of great options for traveling throughout the country. If you're living in a developed area like Seoul, I wouldn't recommend buying a car because of all the traffic jams and difficulty in finding parking spaces. However, if you're living out in the rural areas of the country where public transportation is not as accessible, then you should definitely buy a car.

제 생각에는 당신의 필요에 따라 달라질 것 같은데 한국에서 자동차를 사는 것이 필수라고 물어보면 아니라고 대답할 것입니다. 왜냐하면 전국 어디를 가든 훌륭한 대체 대중교통 수단이 있기 때문입니다. 또한 서울 같이 복잡한 도시에서 살게 된다면 역시 추천하지 않습니다. 항상 차가 막히고 주차구역을 찾는 것이 힘들기 때문입니다. 그러나 대중교통 접근이 어려운 교외지역에 산다면 그때는 자동차를 사야 합니다.

Possible follow up question:

In Korea, there is a large important tax on foreign made cars. What is your opinion of this?

한국에서는 수입차에 대해 큰 세금을 부과합니다. 이것에 대해 어떻게 생각합니까?

I think it's bad for consumers but good for car manufacturers like Hyundai because it makes consumers want to buy Korean made cars for the cheaper price. Personally, I wish we didn't have the import tax because if foreign made cars get cheaper, Korean manufacturers will have to lower their own prices to stay competitive. In the end, I can buy a car for less money.

제 생각에는 소비자에게 나쁜 것 같습니다. 그러나 현대 같은 자동차 회사들에게는 좋은 것입니다. 왜냐하면 소비자들이 저렴한 가격으로 국산차를 구입하게 만드니깐요. 개인적으로 수입차에 대한 세금은 없어야 한다고 생각합니다. 왜냐하면 수입차들 가격이 저렴해지면 국산차들은 경쟁을 위해 가격을 떨어뜨릴 것이기 때문입니다. 결국에 저는 차를 싼 가격에 살 수 있으니깐요

Q5 Overall Fluency

Compare the two locations pictured, describing the similarities and differences.

두 지역의 사진을 비고하교 비슷한점과 다른 점을 묘사해주세요.

(Main) The first picture is of a sandy beach. The second picture is of a pool. (D1) Both pictures represents a place where you can go to swim recreationally. (D2) The difference is that the beach is a part of nature with salt water and waves. On the other hand, the pool water is chlorinated and has no waves. (A) If I had to choose a place to relax, I'd probably choose the beach but if I wanted to swim, I'd probably choose the pool because sand won't get in my eyes.

(Main) 첫번째 사진은 바다 모래 해변이고 두번째 사진은 수영장 입니다.
(D1) 사진 두개 모두 기분 전환으로 수영하러 갈 수 있는 대표석인 상소입니다.
(D2) 다른 점은 해변은 소금물과 파도가 함께 하는 자연의 일부이고 수영장은 염화소독된 물이며 파도가 없습니다.
(A)만약에 쉬고 싶은 곳을 선택하라고 하면 해변을 선택할 것입니다. 그러나 만약 수영을 하고 싶은 곳을 선택하라고 하면 수영장을 선택할 것입니다 왜냐하면 눈에 모래가 들어가지 않을테니까요.

SPA Vocabulary

Must Know SPA Vocab List: Nouns

1. passenger — 승객
2. advantage — 장점
3. disadvantage — 단점
4. similarity — 유사성
5. difference — 차이
6. gesture — 몸짓
7. opinion — 의견
8. occassion — 계기
9. true — 사실
10. false — 거짓
11. rule — 규칙
12. accident — 사고
13. charity — 자선
14. stocks — 주식
15. investment — 투자
16. popular — 인기
17. profitable — 수익성
18. collection — 수집
19. adventure — 모험
20. leisure — 여가
21. appliance — 가전기기
22. trend — 추세
23. percentage — 퍼센트
24. obesity — 비만
25. transportation — 교통
26. authority — 기관
27. route — 경로
28. strike — 파업
29. aspect — 측면
30. misbehavior — 나쁜 품행
31. council — 평의회
32. campaign — 캠페인
33. association — 협회
34. situation — 상황
35. achievement — 달성
36. accomplishment — 성취
37. military — 군대
38. tradition — 전통
39. relationship — 관계
40. organization — 조직
41. advertisement — 광고
42. location — 위티
43. deadline — 마감
44. overnight — 하룻밤
45. compensation — 보상
46. foreign — 외국
47. abroad — 해외
48. instinct — 본능
49. endeavor — 노력
50. fatigue — 피로

Must Know SPA Vocab List: Verbs

1. require — 필요하다
2. bargain — 거래하다
3. bond — 채권하다
4. avoid — 피하다
5. complain — 불평하다
6. exchange — 교환하다
7. provide — 제공하다
8. describe — 설명하다
9. recover — 복구하다
10. prepare — 준비하다
11. develop — 개발하다
12. invest — 투자하다
13. influence — 영향을 미치다
14. immigrate — 이민가다
15. profit — 이익을 내다
16. enforce — 적용하다
17. rent — 임대하다
18. explore — 탐구하다
19. consider — 고려하다
20. alert — 경고하다
21. ban — 금지하다
22. resolve — 해결하다
23. transform — 변환하다
24. undergo — 받다
25. deny — 거부하다
26. propose — 제안하다
27. compensate — 보상받다
28. register — 등록하다
29. operate — 운영하다
30. appreciate — 감사하다
31. divorce — 이혼하다
32. honor — 명예롭다
33. support — 지원하다
34. gamble — 도박하다
35. distract — 혼란스럽다
36. announce — 발표하다
37. regret — 후회하다
38. demand — 수용하다
39. argue — 주장하다
40. strike — 공격하다
41. affect — 영향을 미치다
42. express — 명시하다
43. submit — 제출하다
44. withdraw — 꺼내다
45. serve — 봉사하다
46. control — 제어하다
47. react — 반응하다
48. outline — 윤곽을 그리다
49. increase — 증가하다
50. reduce — 감소하다

Must Know SPA Vocab List: Adjectives, Adverbs, Prepositions

Adjectives		Adverbs		Prepositions	
1. illegal	불법	1. personally	개인적으로	1. before	전
2. bargain	매매	2. slowly	천천히	2. after	후
3. memorable	기억에남는	3. quickly	신속하게	3. later	나중에
4. interior	내부	4. rapidly	빠르게	4. earlier	이전
5. exterior	외부	5. rarely	드물게	5. beside	옆에
6. effective	효과적인	6. illegally	불법적으로	6. above	위의
7. impulsive	충동	7. commonly	일반적으로	7. below	아래
8. valuable	가치	8. strictly	엄격하게	8. next to	다음에
9. thoughtful	사려깊은	9. currently	현재는	9. aside	옆
10. common	일반	10. presently	현재	10. inside	내부
11. rare	드문	11. vaguely	막연히	11. outside	외부
12. successful	성공	12. positively	긍정적	12. top	최고
13. strict	엄격한	13. adversely	악영향	13. bottom	바닥
14. vague	막연한	14. extremely	매우	14. since	이후
15. transparent	투명	15. traditionally	전통적으로	15. across	에서
16. positive	긍정적인	16. approximately	약	16. behind	뒤에
17. adverse	부작용	17. eventually	결국	17. near	근처
18. flexible	유연한	18. naturally	자연	18. despite	불구하고
19. unnecessary	불필요한	19. certainly	확실히	19. except	를 제외한
20. useful	유용한	20. conditionally	조건	20. over	이상/위의
21. famous	유명한	21. finally	마지막으로	21. through	를 통해
22. renowned	유명한	22. primarily	주로	22. about	에 대한
23. ideal	이상	23. significantly	크게	23. beyond	이상
24. modest	겸손	24. automatically	자동	24. upon	에 따라
25. jealous	질투	25. absolutely	절대적으로	25. throughout	에 걸쳐

Transition Phrases to Boost your SPA Score

Linking phrases

1. For example,
There are several ways I can improve my health. For example, I can ride my bike to work instead of driving my car.

2. For instance,
Korea has a variety of exotic foods for tourists to try. For instance, sannakji, otherwise known as live octopus, is exotic to many foreigners.

3. Furthermore,
Studies have shown that eating bananas can help boost your memory. Furthermore, they are also proven to help boost your immune system.

4. Moreover,
Traveling by airplane is the fastest mode of transportation available to travelers. Moreover, air travel has been proven to be safer than traveling by car.

5. In addition,
There are several ways I can improve my health. For example, I can ride my bike to work instead of driving my car. In addition, I can eat fruit instead of potato chips when I want to have a snack.

Compare and Contrast

1. Conversely,
Football is the most popular sport in America. Conversely, cricket is hardly followed there.

2. On the other hand,
Fish is a healthy source of protein. Pork, on the other hand, is considered somewhat unhealthy.

3. However,
John felt very sick today. However, he still went to work.

4. Nevertheless,
Passing the exam is difficult. Nevertheless, with dedicated studying, it is possible.

5. In contrast,
The use of email to send important letters is becoming more and more widespread. In contrast, hand-written letters are hardly sent anymore.

How to Study for the SPA?

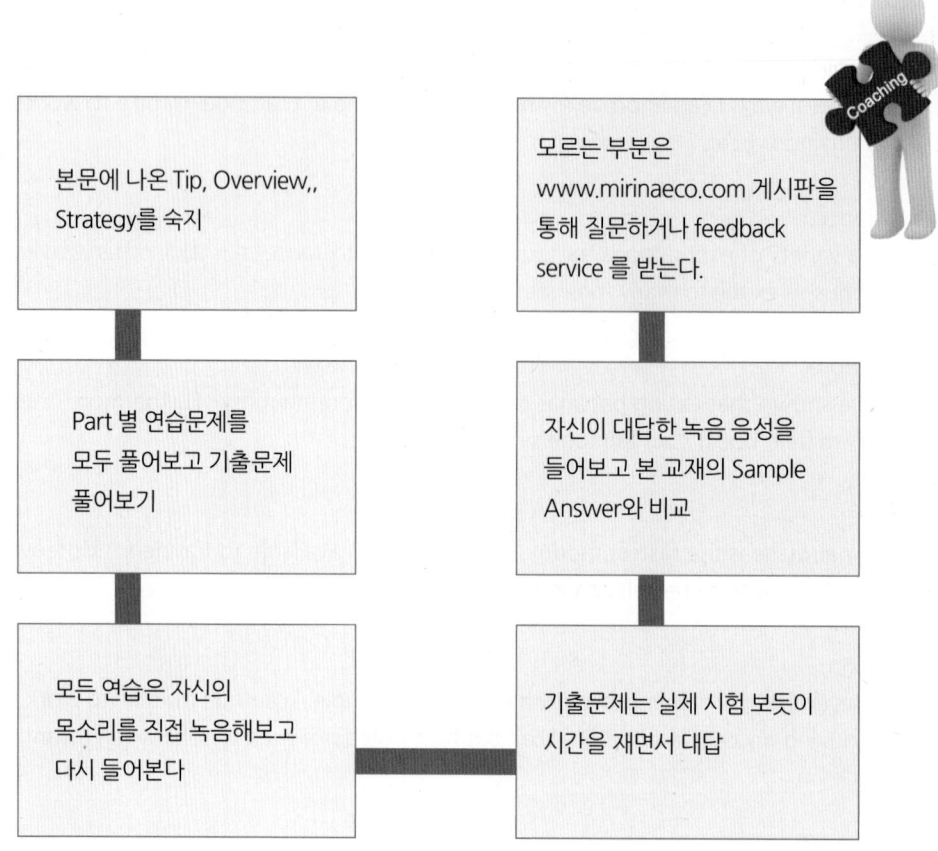

Feedback Service
SPA 전문강사와 원하는 시간에 Coaching을 받아 본다.

Online 모의 Test
Skype를 통해 10분간 Test 실시 후 20분간 피드백을 바로 받아 볼 수 있습니다.

* 모든 서비스는 www.mirinaeco.com에서 회원등록 후 가능합니다.

문의: contact@mirinaeco.com / 070-8242-5411

Memo

Memo